The Hole in the Sheet

Books by Evelyn Kaye

The Parents' Going-Away Planner, with J. Gardner

Write and Sell Your TV Drama! with A. Loring

Relationships in Marriage and the Family, with Professors Stinnett & Walters

Crosscurrents; Children, Families & Religion

How to Treat TV with TLC: The ACT Guide to Children's Television

The Family Guide to Cape Cod, with B. Chesler

The Family Guide to Children's Television

Action for Children's Television (Editor)

THE HOLE
IN THE
SHEET

A Modern Woman Looks at Orthodox and Hasidic Judaism

By Evelyn Kaye

Lyle Stuart Inc.   *Secaucus, New Jersey*

Published by Lyle Stuart Inc.
120 Enterprise Ave., Secaucus, N.J. 07094
Published simultaneously in Canada by
Musson Book Company,
A division of General Publishing Co. Limited
Don Mills, Ontario

Address queries regarding rights and permissions
to Lyle Stuart Inc., 120 Enterprise Ave.,
Secaucus, N.J. 07094

Manufactured in the United States of America

Library of Congress Cataloging-in-Publication Data

Kaye, Evelyn, 1937-
    The hole in the sheet.

    Bibliography: p.
    1. Women in Judaism.   2. Orthodox Judaism—
Controversial literature.   3. Hasidism—Controversial
literature.   4. Sex role—Religious aspects—Judaism.
I. Title.
BM729.W6K39   1987   296.8′32′088042   87-9940
ISBN 0-8184-0437-X

Dedicated to Jewish women who feel anger at the sexist discrimination of Orthodox Judaism, and in special memory of Malke Lee, a Yiddish poet, whose pious father burned all her work because he believed it was against God's will for a girl to write.

Contents

The Hole in the Sheet

1

Introduction: Why Orthodox Judaism Doesn't Like Women

This was a difficult book to write, and it's probably going to upset a great many people who don't like to hear critical comments about Judaism. On the other hand, if you're a woman who has experienced any kind of discrimination at the hands of the Orthodox or Hasidic men who rule the roost, you may feel a sense of liberation that at last someone is going to tell it like it is.

I know what it's like. I grew up in an Orthodox community. I know that when I was born my father said, "What a shame, it's a girl." I know that there were no ceremonies to welcome my arrival within the community. I know that no matter how hard I worked in Hebrew school and how many prizes I won, it didn't really matter. At the age of thirteen, only the boys would have the official ceremony of the Bar Mitzva, which welcomed them into the world of men. And I have spent hours in synagogue sitting watching the men read from the scrolls, organize the services, and ignore the women completely.

I know that the only acceptable role for a Nice Orthodox

Girl is to Get Married and Settle Down, and have several children as soon as possible.

In all the studying and the research and the learning that I've done over the years, I've found that very little has changed. The views of the Orthodox and the Hasidic Jews are as rigidly insulting to women today as they were hundreds of years ago when they were first conceived.

The total separation of men and women in religious services is a reflection of a time when women were considered unworthy of participation in official ceremonies. In the 1830s in this country it was forbidden for men and women to attend meetings together. Two sisters, Angelina and Sarah Grimke, who spoke out against slavery in the 19th century, were also the first to address "promiscuous audiences," where men and women sat together, as we do today. But the Orthodox attitudes have not changed.

In primitive communities, women are considered unclean when they experience their monthly period. They are separated from the rest of the population and not allowed to perform their normal functions. Today, there is no question that menstruation is simply one part of women's lives while they manage to do a great many things at the same time.

The Orthodox attitudes have not changed. They still treat women as unclean objects and have set up a detailed array of laws indicating how they may behave during this time.

And so it goes in a range of behavior, which today is a sign of the freedom for women which the Orthodox would like to curtail.

Sadly, there's no way Orthodox Judaism or Hasidism can adjust to the present without making radical changes in their attitudes toward women. Because this is the century of the New Revolution for Women. We didn't ask for all of it. But it has happened.

Since the beginning of this century, there have been dramatic changes in women's lives:

POLITICS: For the first time ever, women have the right to vote, to run for elected office, to serve at local, state and national levels of appointment, and to be involved in political decision-making.

EDUCATION: For the first time ever, all women have an opportunity to be educated to the same level as men. They go to school as children, they may go on to university, they may study for a profession, they may continue their education.

WORK: For the first time ever, women have access to the world of work, with openings in a broad range of positions often completely closed off in the past. They earn money, they make investments, they buy goods and services, they pay taxes, they own homes.

FAMILY: For the first time ever, women can choose when and if to have children, using safe and reliable methods of birth control. They can limit the size of their families. They can decide to be childless. They can conceive by new chemical methods.

HEALTH: For the first time ever, the discoveries and developments in health care have benefited women enormously. They rarely die in childbirth, nor do they develop diseases or "women's complaints." Their children are protected by vaccinations and other health discoveries. They live longer and have more active lives.

HOUSEWORK: For the first time ever, machines have eased the burden of drudgery which most women accepted for centuries. The refrigerator, washing machine, dryer, dishwasher, vacuum and other tools of housework have made it simpler to keep homes clean, and cut the hours it used to take to be a housekeeper.

CHOICES: For the first time ever, women can make choices in their lives. Less than a hundred years ago, a woman had one option: marriage-and-motherhood. She was considered a liability, a failure, an object of pity if she did not achieve that status. Today, women work, marry, have children, travel, go to outer space, become presidents, create music and art, win Olympic events, solve world problems.

A revolution has a kaleidoscopic effect. Everything gets shaken up and nothing looks the same any more. Both men and women have to adjust to the changes in women's lives. For some people it's easier than for others. But traditional religions decided to play ostrich. They've stuck their heads in the sand and pretended nothing has happened at all.

Why Orthodox Judaism Is Stuck

Orthodox Judaism is the patriarchal, all-male traditional branch of Judaism, from which Hasidism is an offshoot. Both groups follow the ancient biblical laws, and believe that the modern world has nothing to teach the rabbis who laid down the rules hundreds of years ago. If life today seems to contradict some of those teachings, they simply twist the teachings around to fit.

In contrast, modern Reform Judaism, which began in the 1800s, recognized the deep-rooted changes of our times, and adjusted to the realities.

For example, the old law said that the Sabbath day was a day of rest. No one should work, not even the animals who served the farmer. We're talking about a time when the Jews were tilling the soil and living the simple life of an agrarian community. So their donkeys, mules and maybe the camels would rest on the Sabbath day. No one rode anywhere.

Today, few Jews actually work in farming. There aren't too many work animals around. Even the farmers have moved on to tractors. But the persnickety minds of the rabbinate have interpreted the old laws to mean that even today you still must not ride anywhere. You must not take a train, ride a bus, drive a car, or fly on a plane. If it was work to take out a donkey in the 4th century, it's work to catch a subway in the 20th century.

There are unlimited rules about not riding on the Sabbath, and it's a point of intense discussion for the Orthodox.

For the Reform community, the issue is not an important one. There is no prohibition against travelling on the Sabbath, though the day is respected as a day of rest.

But for the Orthodox, the issue of travelling on the Sabbath is a critical gauge of Jewishness on the scale of good to bad.

Assuming you decide *not* to travel, which is "good," you then have to worry about the sub-rules. For example, there are passionate discussions about what you may carry while walking on the Sabbath. If you are carrying something, you are causing it to travel, and therefore may be actually doing work. The Orthodox go to great lengths to tie their handkerchiefs around their waists (pockets are not good enough) and make sure they wear their gloves all the time so they don't carry them by accident. It's not done to take a bag with you, because then you're carrying all over again.

There are more rules about how far you can walk on the Sabbath day. (Of course there are rules about everything you can think of. There are even rules about what you may think about when you are sitting on the toilet.) However, if you put up a boundary, you can carry things because you are then in a specially designated area. So Orthodox Jews in one New York area fought a major battle over erecting a special barrier around their community so that people could walk and carry things on the Sabbath. It's just like creating a temporary ghetto.

For me, it's the rules about women which are the most offensive. A little girl is invisible. No ceremonies welcome her arrival. No one recognizes a mother's achievement in giving birth. No traditions exist to celebrate girls.

Women sit behind screens in synagogue services, or behind curtains, or half-screens, or upstairs, or sometimes separately in another room. They never take an active part in the services. They are never called to read from the scrolls of the law, the essential reason for the service. They receive no public recognition.

For the men, the synagogue provides a forum of appreciation throughout life. At the Bar Mitzva, a boy is the center of attention. As a young man, he is welcomed to services and called up to read from the scroll at times of achievement, such as qualifying as a lawyer or getting engaged. When his children are born, he is again given honors during the service, perhaps designated to carry the scrolls around the synagogue. And older men, longtime members, are often honored for the birth of a grandchild or for reaching the age of

70 or 80, or on their retirement from a volunteer community activity.

Women have milestones in their lives too. But no one ever recognized the mother's role during a service. No one ever chose to give an honor to a woman who had qualified as a teacher. And certainly no one took any notice of a widow whose grandchild had been born, or who had retired after years of service to the women's committees or the synagogue offices.

This discrimination extends to the role of women in Orthodox law. A woman cannot testify in court, and cannot affix her signature as a witness, even on a marriage contract.

One Israeli woman reported:

"The rabbi in the office of the rabbinate wouldn't let me be a witness for my friend's wedding license because, as he so nicely put it, 'Women are light-headed.' "

This blanket condemnation of women's abilities is one of the fundamental beliefs of the Orthodox and Hasidic creed.

The Lubavitcher Hasidic movement, which is by far the best known Hasidic sect and especially zealous in converting Jews to their own extreme form of Judaism, has distributed a leaflet about the role of women, explaining why they cannot have legal status:

"A woman has been gifted with an extra measure of natural emotion. But an overly measure of emotionalism is a hindrance in legal matters. ... The average woman is more emotional so the woman had to be disqualified from judgeship and similar legal matters. Man is less emotional and can be more objective."

It sounds like the kind of arguments which used to be put forward against the right of women to vote.

Orthodox and Hasidic Jews like to promote the idea of a Jew as an old, bearded man wearing black, perhaps with a prayer shawl thrown devoutly around his shoulders.

But that's one small image of what Jews are like. There are thousands of Jews who don't look the least bit like that, and among the men, women and children who are Jewish that stereotype is completely out of date.

When I was growing up I used to try to find pictures or

drawings of girls and women in Jewish books so that I could find someone who looked like me. I certainly couldn't imagine turning out like one of the bearded rabbis.

But there never seemed to be drawings of lively, energetic young girls running or climbing or doing any of the things I liked to do. Instead, they were always cooking or cleaning or sitting quietly at the table, listening to the men who prayed.

I recently saw a photograph of a Hasidic celebration for the anniversary of the rabbinic scholar, Maimonides. Again, I found myself looking at the newsprint on the page trying to find someone who might look like me, a grown woman and a mother. But along the rows and rows of blackbearded men with dark hats and white faces I didn't see a single woman. Once again, they had simply disappeared, as if they didn't exist at all.

That's how the extreme Orthodox and Hasidic men like to have their women. They believe that women are wicked, unreliable, sexual temptresses, who are put on earth to lead men into evil ungodly ways and tempt them to stop observing the laws and commandments of Judaism.

Women are not human beings, able to cope with the demands of real life. They are strange people who must be bound by stern rules so that they know what to do, and who must be kept strictly within bounds, lest they upset the established male order.

When I walk past the Hasidic Jews on the streets of New York, I feel them avoid me as I pass. It's rather like being a leper. They do not allow their wives to walk alone anywhere. The women are tied to the home and community, bound by persistent teachings of their inferiority and their inability to do anything on their own.

Their only role is to produce children, and bring them up. But what happens when their child-rearing years are over? Do they transform themselves instantly into grandmothers? Do they never ask themselves who they are? Is their individuality simply wiped away, as if they do not exist?

In the past, many women endured a life of semi-slavery, caring for demanding husbands and unlimited children. Now, for the first time in history, we have a choice we can make. The religious extremists are intent on denying us choices.

Orthodox and Hasidic Jews refuse to allow women to read from the scrolls of the Law, to take part in services, or to train to become a rabbi. The Conservative and Reform and Reconstructionist groups have all accepted these roles for women. The Orthodox believe that women's place is firmly in the home, and that they have nothing to learn from the modern world.

But even within the home, their situation is depressingly rooted in centuries past.

The laws of Orthodoxy are fixated on menstruation. Yes, the rabbis are absolutely fascinated by a woman's cycle of reproduction. Like the backward tribes of the world, they are determined to separate these bleeding women from the rest of the community. And they have set up an impenetrable thicket of laws which tell women when they're clean, when they're dirty, and what exactly they may and may not do.

There are rules about what they may touch (not their husbands, when they are menstruating), where they may go (nowhere alone) and with whom they may speak (only Jews).

The Hasidic and Orthodox attitudes dismiss without a word everything this century has taught us about sexuality, about relationships between men and women, and about the intimacy and tenderness of marriage. Strict Jewish laws demand marital sex, which is only for procreation. Masturbation, they say, is forbidden. And during sexual intercourse, there are strict rules about what you may wear, what you must think and how you must behave. The emphasis, as in the era of Victorian prudery, is on "duty," which must be "performed properly."

What's more, the entire event must be carried out in pitch darkness, and at no time must a man look up on his naked wife.

Women are expected to be completely modest and withdrawn, and at no time are they supposed to show themselves without a covering. Since this applies to the time they are actually having intercourse, they have to be especially careful that nothing shows.

Which brings me to the story of The Hole in the Sheet. Personally, I have never seen such a sheet. I do not have any first-hand knowledge of the actual design of such a sheet. But whenever I mention this story to an Orthodox Jew, there's a moment of immediate recognition that this is the way it should happen. Or at least the way the story says it should happen.

In order to protect the modesty of the wife during intercourse, a sheet is kept between her and her husband, with a hole at the appropriate place for the correct connection to be made.

If you want to be an outstanding Jew, and if you want to make sure that you see nothing at all, I'm sure that the sheet is probably the best idea. However, human nature is notoriously weak, and who knows but in a moment of unexpected passion even the most Orthodox of the Orthodox may throw the sheet aside? On the other hand, perhaps they don't.

What disturbs me is the thinking behind these customs. It's a denial that the woman is a person, needing human contact and sensitive consideration. It's pretending that only the connection matters. It's denying any opportunity for exploration, for delight, for spontaneity, for mutual sharing of experiences.

The Orthodox treat all relationships between the sexes as if they might lead to contamination by contact. From the earliest days, boys and girls are separated. Detailed instructions of what girls must wear to cover themselves up apply from the age of three. There are strict rules about the age a boy may be with a girl alone, or a girl with a boy.

And in meeting and marrying, among the most extreme the system is as rigid as arranging marriages in the Orient. A man and woman may meet three times, with another person present on every occasion. After that, the man will decide if he wants to marry, or else he will never see the woman again.

After a strictly segregated wedding ceremony, the two follow the intricate rules for when intercourse may take place. This can only be at certain times, related to a woman's menstrual cycle, and after a week's clean period and her visit to the ritual bath. Naturally, this coincides with the time of ovulation when a woman is most likely to become pregnant.

It's a blueprint for keeping women pregnant and tied to the home. The extremists in Judaism as in other faiths understand that allowing women to control their fertility gives them an independence and power which fearful men cannot accept. Under the guise of religion, men have trapped women once again in the treadmill of childcare, pregnancy and housework, dependent on the goodwill of their husbands.

The Impossible Balance

Some modern women like to say they can balance their careers, their professions, their involvement in the world of today with the demands of their religion. I admire them. But I think it's the road to feminist schizophrenia.

The reason for much of the discrimination is the background of the people who interpreted the laws. They were all men, all who lived hundreds of years ago, and who would have certainly strongly opposed giving women the vote.

What's more, over the years, the kinds of segregation which are accepted in Orthodox and Hasidic communities have become more and more extreme.

Take a look back in the Bible to the years when Moses was leading the children of Israel out of Egypt toward the land of Israel. At that time no one wore long black coats or had long sidecurls. Those arrived with the Hasidic movement about 1750. No one demanded that the women walk separately from the men as they searched the desert for the manna from Heaven. That came in the anti-woman stance of the rabbinic interpretations in the early years when the laws were codified into the Talmud. And no one forbade women from taking a position of leadership. Miriam, Moses' sister, was one of the recognized leaders of the long trek, together with his brother Aaron.

Repressing women to positions of inferiority came from the deeply felt disdain for women by the rabbis who interpreted the laws Moses received.

These attitudes reflect the disdain for all new ideas which permeates Orthodox and Hasidic Judaism. But there's another and more disturbing sign. The community has developed an insular, single-minded approach which is completely intolerant of any views that differ from its own.

In the past, intolerance and intra-tribal fighting was a constant refrain in Biblical stories. The Jews have always been an argumentative and contentious people. But when such battles were kept within the ghetto or within the community, the problems were isolated. Today, the world has shrunk, and intolerance is far more dangerous than before.

When Orthodox Jews disagree with Conservative Jews or with Reform Jews today, the reactions are far ranging. The dissent has wide implications. And their angry refusal to consider compromises may lead to a confrontation no other branch of Judaism would even contemplate.

Let me give you an example of this intolerance, which took place in 1985. A young boy, whose grandparents had escaped from Poland to America, was approaching his 13th birthday and his Bar Mitzva ceremony. A member of the Reform congregation, he told his rabbi, who happened to be a woman, about his interest in his Polish ancestors. She happened to find out that one community in Poland had not seen a Bar Mitzva for forty years, because there were no young Jews left.

She managed to contact the rabbi, and suggested that the boy have his Bar Mitzva in Poland at the community's synagogue in tribute to his grandparents.

Whatever the time and the tribulations and the organization took, she managed to put it together. The ceremony was arranged, the boy's family arrived in Poland, and the event was prepared, according to the Reform tradition in which he had been raised.

Comes now the voice of the Orthodox Jew. When the community saw what was happening, and how it was being set up, they protested that the Bar Mitzva was not a Real Bar Mitzva because it was not Orthodox. What's more they brought over your basic 16th century model rabbi (old, bearded, long black coat) and he took over the service. He even attempted to send the woman rabbi to sit in the separate women's section.

To his credit, the Bar Mitzva Boy protested and she was allowed to stand by him, while the Orthodox rabbi ran the proceedings. No one protested. No one said, "This is scandalous! This is wrong! This is unjust!" Just imagine if the set-up had been the other way around. If an Orthodox rabbi had had the imagination to organize the Bar Mitzva in Poland, and then a Reform rabbi had burst in and taken over, especially if she had been a woman. Now that would have been a brouhaha.

But the Orthodox would not have thought of such an imaginative and co-operative venture. The essence of the Orthodox approach is isolation. The ideal situation is one in which all the community lives together, and no one around holds any beliefs different from the accepted views. It's very difficult to find any tolerance, understanding, recognition of the rights of others to believe what they choose, or respect for different religious ideas among Orthodox or Hasidic Jews.

I know that the same rigidity is found in many religious groups. There are fundamentalist Protestant sects, extremist Catholics and sects like the Hare Krishna that have taken Eastern religions to extreme boundaries of belief and observance.

But since the Orthodox Jewish community is the one in which I grew up, I can only speak with authority about that experience.

The intolerance so clearly expressed by the Orthodox during the Bar Mitzva ceremony is reflected in every aspect of their lives. They do not want to mix with non-Orthodox Jews. They avoid meeting non-Jews completely. They never have any contact with blacks, Hispanics or the many other communities who live in cities with large Jewish populations. And they take a positive delight in not knowing anything about what is happening in the world outside their narrow perspective. It's as if their ignorance will protect them from facing change.

They are not interested in finding an acceptable compromise so that they might be able to drink a glass of water in the non-Orthodox home. They delight in embarrassing others to show their own extremist behavior and observances. And they do not hesitate to assert that they and God have Judaism quite monopolized, and everyone else is absolutely wrong.

I always imagine what their faces will look like on the Day of Judgment, when God looks down from Her heavenly cloud and points out that the true way of the Jew is to work on a communal farm in Israel, and live in a way which gives women total equality with men.

After all, it's important to remember that all the present versions of Heaven and Hell have been written by men.

From all that I have read, researched and studied, I am quite certain that the Orthodox and Hasidic Jews are unequivocally wrong in their interpretations of Judaism. There are as many laws preaching tolerance and fairness as there are laws advocating segregation and isolation. There are as many injunctions to respect the beliefs of others and their feelings as there are demands to observe outlandish practices relating to behavior. And there are enough examples of change within Jewish history to show that those who recognize the rights of women and adjust the patterns of observance are perfectly correct in their interpretations.

Why the Dangers Are So Important Today

We are living in a time when the world is constantly shrinking. We can fly from one side of the continent to the other in hours. We can zoom along highways in minutes. We can speed across the water to distant lands in a few days.

The essential change for women is that we are now firmly a part of the world. From the days when we sat demurely at one side, living our lives vicariously through our fathers, our brothers and our husbands, and then later through our children, we have at last found our own voice and our own lives.

In all the countries of the world where the New Revolution for Women has taken place, the changes are amazing. Women are educated, women work in responsible positions, women are active in political decisions, women help other women and men to share in their knowledge and expertise, women travel freely to wherever they want to go.

But in all those countries that refuse to acknowledge the dramatic changes, women are living as they did for centuries past. They have no education, they do not find jobs outside their homes, they wear garments which men demand they put on, they have no place in politics, they are denied the right to travel, they are kept firmly in the background. The contrast is distressingly vivid. It's visible in those countries under the repressive regime of extreme Muslim rulers. It's visible in extreme Catholic countries. And it's clear in those communities under extreme Orthodox Jewish leadership.

I have no particularly high regard for religion in the lives of women. I feel strongly that most religious teachings demean women, demand adherence to the laws and behavior dictated by men and ignore the positive contributions women have made to the world.

From what I have seen of the attitudes of those who lead major religious groups, they'd like to enforce the rules which keep men in charge and allow women a minimal amount of authority without permitting them to make too many changes.

They keep propagating the myth that a family is somehow uniquely perfect if it has a mother and a father, and some children. That has never been true. There have been widowed mothers who brought up children perfectly well without men. There have been men who quite deliberately left their wives to manage alone. There have been women left economically destitute by men who had no interest in supporting their families.

These backwards-looking religious extremists want to deprive women of the right to education. They want to persuade women that they are incapable of coping in the world outside the home. They want them to believe that having dozens of children is some kind of religious duty. They want to see them captive in the home again, coping with the thousand and one demands of children, housekeeping and looking after their husbands, just as the Bible says.

These attitudes threaten to destroy all that women have gained in this century. And, what is more, they could force women back into lives of drudgery, cruelty, helplessness and boredom, where they will be eternal servants to the men who hold the power.

Let's take a look at how that is starting to happen today. The Hasidic and Orthodox communities are opening more and more schools which teach the essentials of the conformist approach. A generation of children is growing up without meeting children from any other background but their own. They are learning about the world from one perspective only. And though we live in a multi-racial, multi-ethnic and extraordinarily rich and diverse community of cultures, a new generation is growing up believing that everything must be inferior to the dictates of Orthodox and Hasidic Judaism.

The emphasis of Orthodox and Hasidic approaches vary in intensity in their approach toward a woman's role. But the core issue is clear: women are supposed to be wives and mothers, bringing up their children full time. Perhaps now and then they may be able to do a little something here and there. But the only value they have within the community is as wife and mother. This is a tragedy today. For the first time, women have choices. And, despite the best of myths, some women don't like children and are happier living without them. What's more, some marriages are happier without children too. And, finally, it's clear the economic tenor of the times demands that women can contribute to the family earnings. It may be the only way for a family to survive in the future.

The issue of financial security is a crucial point. Economic necessity is the reason so many women are now working outside the home. The costs of housing, of food and of shoes and clothes have soared, and for most families two incomes are needed for survival.

None of these points penetrate beneath the thick black hats of the ultra-Orthodox.

They simply go on behaving as if the present did not exist, and we're still skipping about on the ice of the frozen ghettos of middle Poland two hundred years ago.

Already, the trend of the future is becoming clear. We are raising a generation of Jewish paupers.

Take a look at an enclave of Hasidic Jews who reside in a small town near New York City.

Few of them have working skills. They live a restricted existence, yet loudly assert their religious demands. However, it turns out that seventy percent of them—almost three quarters of the entire population—receive some form of public assistance, such as Medicaid, food stamps or welfare. The average number of children in each family is 6.6.

That's the obvious pattern which will become more and more common. If you refuse to allow women to limit births, if you refuse to allow them to learn how to qualify for a job, and if you deny them the right for any role outside the family, you are dooming them to permanent poverty. The equation is crystal clear—and has been proved time and time again:

No education = No Job = Poverty.

A friend told me an interesting story about what's happening. Two well-educated young people met and married. They became infatuated with extreme Orthodox observance, and determined that they would go to Israel. They both agreed that birth control was unacceptable. She would have children, and not in any way use her college education in computer sciences. She stayed home and had five children in five years. He managed to find a position as a rabbi-teacher, earning some money.

One day, he received a letter from an old girlfriend in London. He decided he wanted to see her, and flew off. He discovered that he liked being in London, liked being away from his five children, and wrote home that he was giving up his wife and children and moving in with his girlfriend.

Despite letters and pleading phone calls, he refused to return. His wife was devastated. Yet within the community she had chosen to live, she had only few resources: charity, and pity. She was given some money from the synagogue, and a few women used to come round and bring her food and clothes.

It's important to bear in mind that this is happening in the 20th century. This is a woman who had a good education, who had access to birth control information, who had choices. But we're dealing with someone caught inside the total craziness of Orthodox teachings. She has given up her mind in exchange for the fairy stories about Judaism and its teachings. She has allowed herself to become as helpless as any peasant woman living in the backwoods of central Africa. And she believes that this is good for her.

The tragedy is that this scenario will be repeated, time and time again, if the teachings of the Hasidim and the extreme Orthodox are not challenged. There will be more and more women living in helpless poverty, showing their daughters how to be weak and submissive, and depriving their children of education and skills to survive.

Orthodox and Hasidic Judaism likes to assert that it is the only way, the only path and the only truthful interpretation of Judaism.

I will prove in the pages ahead, that these attitudes are destructive, detrimental and discriminatory to women, and will bring misery and unhappiness to the next generations. The Reform and more liberal branches of Judaism are teaching the true interpretation of the faith.

For the Orthodox communities to deny the changes in women's lives is to deny the major revolution of our times. It's like King Canute sitting at the edge of the seashore, and waving his hands to stop the waves breaking against his feet. The king realized his mistake, and quickly moved back on to dry ground before he was washed out to sea.

But will the leaders of the Orthodox and Hasidic communities today want to save the women stranded at the seashore? Or will their blinkered, narrow-minded views persuade them that it's better to let a few women drown in the sea than to give up their belief that faith can stop the waves?

2

An Incredibly Short Background to Judaism

Let's turn time backwards in its flight. Let's show the steps which led to the impasse of the 20th century.

Judaism has never stood rigidly still. In every generation there have been new developments. Every century chooses to focus on different issues. And every community argues, squabbles, disagrees and disapproves in significant and individual styles.

A classic Jewish joke is about the two Jews who are stranded on a desert island. They build three synagogues; one for each of them, and one they would never set foot in.

At different times in history, women's roles were not the least bit like the modern Jewish housewife's. But I will show that the rules by which today's Orthodox women live were established to meet situations which don't exist today. And that to persist in trying to make them fit is like trying to tuck an elephant into a suitcase.

According to Jewish calculations, 1986 is 5747, because Judaism's history began over 5,000 years ago, in the days of Abraham. He is credited as being the first man to conceive of the mind-boggling idea that there was only one God, invisible, indivisible, all-powerfull and unique. That discovery is part of the literature of the Jewish, Moslem and Christian faiths.

In those times, people lived simple farming lives without the benefit of electronic media to flash the news by satellite in an instant.

We only know about Abraham from the Bible, which was written long after his death by men who wanted to record the stories which had been passed down orally for many years. And we also don't know how accurate the Bible really is. There aren't any sources cited, or easily accessible contemporary accounts of the same events with which to compare the details.

The Bible likes to present history as a series of family stories such as that of the two sons of Adam and Eve, Cain and Abel, who were jealous of each other. Or of the family of Abraham and Sarah, and their son, Isaac, born late in their lives, and almost sacrificed to God. That's why the Bible is so fascinating. It's about human beings who know the same feelings and emotions we experience today. But it makes it difficult to pinpoint the exact details of when and how significant historical events took place. There are no theological discussions, and the many commentaries were added later.

It's generally agreed that those who accepted Abraham's ideas about one God became the first Jews. At that time it was normal to have an abundance of different gods, who might be animals, stones, spirits, the sun, the moon, birds. People worshipped as many as they wanted. The Jews, with this new idea of an unseen God who saw all and wanted His people to lead honorable lives, were different.

Their numbers multiplied over the years. When Moses was born, the Jews were suffering as slaves. A harsh dictator in Egypt had taken away the rights granted by a previous ruler, and forced the Jews to work as builders and brickmakers.

The change had brought the Jews to a low point in their existence. They had begun to doubt the God who had promised to care for them. The laws set by the stern Pharaoh deprived them of all rights, and forced them to live in poverty.

It was Moses who rescued them. Brought up in the court of Pharaoh by the Pharaoh's daughter, his Jewish conscience had been aroused when he saw an Egyptian beating a Jewish slave. He killed the Egyptian. Then, frightened, he ran away to the desert. There, he saw a bush on fire, but not burning away. When he went closer to the strange phenomenon, God spoke to him from the burning bush, telling him to rescue the Jews from the slavery of Egypt.

Though at first he said he couldn't do it, he finally accepted the task. And it was Moses who led the Jews to the next stage of their development. After the escape from Egypt, much wandering in the wilderness and many adventures, God told Moses the Jews were the Chosen People and would receive God's Law.

The movie versions shows he went up to the top of Mount Sinai and came down with two carved tablets outlining the Ten Commandments. But according to Jewish belief, he received two sets of laws at Sinai:

—the written law, which was the five books of Moses, called the "Torah," including Genesis, Exodus, Leviticus, Numbers and Deuteronomy; and
—the oral law, which was told to Moses and which was handed down orally for many generations, called the "Mishnah."

Moses took the people to the borders of the promised land "flowing with milk and honey," and they settled in Israel for hundreds of years.

They lived by the written laws outlined in the Torah, and in the oral laws passed down from father to son, from religious leader to community, and embellished and changed little by little over the years.

There was no thought of writing down these laws because the Jews lived in a tightly closed community, where there was no difficulty in sharing the stories of the past.

The crisis for the Jews came about 2,000 years ago. War, conquest and persistent attacks came from all sides, and they were driven from their homeland. Scattered among the countries of the Middle East, they began to try and assess what it was that made them Jewish.

From that time until 1947, almost 2,000 years later when Israel was created by a United Nations vote, the Jews were without a land of their own.

They became permanent wanderers, instead of settled farmers. They moved with the tides of tolerance and fled with the waves of repression and persecution. They lived in England until 1250, when a pogrom in York, in the north of England, led to an edict banishing all Jews from the country. They did not return until 1656, when the protectorate of Oliver Cromwell was in power.

They lived for centuries in Spain, becoming doctors, lawyers, musicians, poets, until the passionate Catholicism of Isabella and Ferdinand led to the Spanish Inquisition of the 1400s. Thousands of Jews died, thousands more fled, and thousands adopted Catholicism outwardly to survive while secretly practicing their Judaism; these were called Marranos.

The Jews lived for generations in Europe, until the warped mind of Adolf Hitler unleashed a modern persecution of those who were not born "Aryans." Again, they fled—and many came to the United States.

The Scattered Jews

Once the Jews had been driven out of the promised land and scattered among the peoples of the world, the rabbis were worried they would forget their allegiance to the laws handed down to Moses at Sinai, and their adherence to the beliefs of Abraham.

So between the second and sixth centuries after the dispersal, a book called "The Talmud" was written in two different places, Babylonia and Jerusalem. The Talmud was the written form of the Mishnah, the Oral Law. It's an extensive collection of discussions, interpretations and expositions of the laws and observances, with comments from many rabbis. Today, the Talmud written in Babylonia is the accepted version, and the Jerusalem Talmud is ignored.

Much later, in the 15th century, an outstanding Jewish scholar called Joseph Caro decided to codify the many laws relating to Jewish observance and practice. Between 1488 and 1575 he wrote the "Shulhan Aruch" or "Code of Jewish Law," which is a compilation of all the details of the written and oral versions. That book is available in English and Hebrew, and is the basic reference for Orthodox religious behavior today.

There are plenty of other interpretive works, including a separate "Mishnah Torah," by the scholar Maimonides, and other rabbinic interpretations.

The concept of the "Old Testament" does not exist in Judaism. "The Torah" contains the five books of Moses, and when the rest of the books in the Bible are gathered together, the collection is the "T'nack." That word is made up of the first three Hebrew letters of three parts of this book:

TORAH—meaning the first five books;
NEVEEIM—meaning prophets, whose stories are here;
KETUVIM—meaning writings, such as Ecclesiastes and Proverbs.

The Scrolls of the Law, which are read during synagogue services, contain only the Torah. Each scroll is handwritten in Hebrew letters on parchment. All the religious books are available printed in modern book format, but the tradition of using the scrolls has continued.

There are other religious books which have developed over the years, including the "Siddur," meaning order or arrangement. This is the prayerbook which contains the services for Friday evening, Sabbath, holidays, and special occasions, like the lighting of Hanukkah candles. And there are prayerbooks for the major festivals of the New Year, Day of Atonement, Passover, the Feast of Weeks and Tabernacles.

Individuality is the keynote of Judaism. Different communities in different parts of the world develop individual interpretations and customs. But one thing was unchanging; no women ever wrote, contributed to or was cited individually in any of the religious books of the law. Judaism was created by men.

In the early days of the dispersal, according to Abba Eban, in *Heritage: Civilization and the Jews,* it was rare for a woman to be educated or take an active part in the community or political or religious life.

The laws said that a man could pay off his obligations by selling his daughter into slavery. He was not allowed to do so with his son.

The emphasis on studying the Torah was for boys and men only. The girls and women would defer to the men as long as they did not have access to the same knowledge.

The Jewish laws define certain ritual obligations which total the unlikely number of 613. However, women are exempted from observing many of these, on the assumption that because women would be so busy looking after their children, they would not have time to fulfill their obligations.

Women also are excluded from testifying before a religious court, as are a child and a slave. However, a freed slave may testify.

The attitudes of those who framed and interpreted the laws of Moses heavily flavored their decisions. Women and girls are constantly cast into the role of handmaiden, servant, mother or wife. There's no recognition that women have the right to make their own decisions or take responsibility for their own actions. The basic choices of selecting the path of good or evil were designed for men to make, and women to follow.

The Hasidim

In the 1700s, a man called Baal Shem Tov, in Podolia, a town in central Europe, developed the concept of Hasidim.

At that time there was a rigid adherence to the law as defined in the Code. Israel Baal Shem Tov, an orphan, was brought up in an Orthodox community, and became the beadle of the synagogue. But he decided to leave. With his wife, he retreated into the Carpathian Mountains where he lived for some years.

The Hasidic tradition says that on his thirty-sixth birthday, probably in 1736, he revealed himself as a healer and leader. He expelled demons, performed miracle cures, and presented a completely different view of Judaism to the strict law-keeping of the community.

He believed the true approach to God was through ecstasy and mystic prayer, rather like the Christian sects in which speaking in tongues and other ecstatic experiences are part of worship. He became the first rabbi of the Hasidic movement, and decreed that each rabbi should choose his successor. The second leader, Dov Baer, moved Hasidism from southeast Poland to the center, and it spread throughout the country. Like Christians, the Hasids sent out missionaries to convert other Jews to the ecstasies of the new Judaism.

His rabbis responded to a call from God, and saw their roles as a zealous mission to bring others into the fold.

From the beginning, many rabbis were shocked by the excesses of Hasidism. Hasidic leaders believed that "devekut" or "clinging to God" was the essential aspect of faith. Their prayers incorporated much physical swaying and shaking, shouting and exhortations, in an attempt to show their true "communion with God." Many of them were limited in their knowledge of the Torah, but they felt their passion was more important than their knowledge.

By 1830 the sect had sizable groups of followers in the Ukraine, Galicia and central Poland, as well as Bylorussi-Lithuania and Hungary. The movement came to Europe with immigrants around 1881, and later arrived in the United States.

The main difference between Orthodox Judaism and the Hasidic sect is the use of an intermediary between God and man. The Hasidim believe that the "zaddik" or learned man is the one to intercede between God and the Jewish people, and he is the person the Hasidim must defer to. In Hasidic homes today, there are photos of the present "zaddik," or rabbi-leader, set in a place of honor, rather as paintings of Jesus are often displayed in Catholic homes. Orthodox Jews believe that man may speak directly to God, and that an intermediary distorts basic Jewish beliefs.

Historical records show that many of the practices of the Hasidim, like turning somersaults during prayer, using alcohol, tobacco and other stimulants and similar excesses, were sharply criticized.

In 1786, a traditional Orthodox community in Russia wrote:

"Worthless and wanton men who call themselves Hasidim have deserted the Jewish group and have set up a so-called place of worship for themselves. And thus, as everyone knows, they worship in a most insane fashion, following a different ritual which does not conform to the religion of our holy Torah, and they tread a path our fathers never trod. . . . The exaggerations and stories of miracles described in their books are particularly and evident lies."

Many Jews wrote books critical of the Hasidim. Joseph Perl (1773–1839) wrote *The Revealer of Secrets* in 1819, as a parody of Hasidism, which imitated the sect's pious style so successfully that some Hasidim accepted it as a serious work.

Isaac Baer Levisohn wrote a book called *The Valley of the Dead*. In it, a "zaddik" dies and finds himself in Hell, much to his surprise. He admits that he had no secular learning and no Talmudic knowledge, so he had to become a Hasidic rabbi.

The rabbi-leaders of the group were often less than perfect. A few led lives of luxury, accepted gifts and money from their followers, or used their positions for sexual license. The Maggid of Koznitz (1733–1814) distributed health remedies and amulets with his name on them. And Friedman of Ruzhin (1797–1858) lived in opulence, surrounded by servants, with an elegant carriage and four horses.

However, there was never any doubt about the Hasidic attitude toward women. A Hasid avoids looking at women. If he must talk to a woman, he faces sideways, and he won't shake hands with her.

Surprisingly, there was one woman "zaddik," the "Maid of Ludomir" (1805–1892). She observed the strict separation of the sexes, and used to give her sermons to the Hasidim who followed her from a room adjoining theirs.

But apart from that bizarre exception, women defer to men within Hasidism. Like extreme Orthodox Jews, they are not seen during synagogue services. They do not read from the scrolls of the law. The girls do not have a ceremony at the age of thirteen.

Modern critics of Hasidism find it as difficult as did their predecessors to deal with the ecstatic passion and unquestioning hero worship of the "rebbe" which permeate Hasidic life. And while the clothes the Hasidim wear today may look out of place, they were quite acceptable in the 1700s when the movement spread. The black hats, long coats and heavy shoes are a remnant of middle European culture, just as the simple clothes of the Amish sects of the Mennonite church reflect their determination not to accept modern customs.

Today's Jewish Divisions

In the 18th century in Europe, many aspects of Jewish law had been dropped because they were irrelevant to the life of that time. No one observed the laws relating to the temple services, or the priesthood, or the details of agriculture. The criminal laws were rarely invoked since most criminal cases went before state courts.

Reform

Some Jews felt a need for change to bring practices in line with the practices of the times. Particularly in Germany, where Jews had achieved freedom to receive an education, Jews were becoming a part of society, no longer ostracized.

Between 1810 and 1818, services were often held in German, as well as in Hebrew. Some services were shortened. The music was provided by an organ, and a preacher delivered a sermon in German, instead of the usual Talmudic dissertation in Hebrew or Yiddish.

The early Reform Jews then attacked traditional Jewish education. They set up a number of modern schools modeled on Protestant schools to expand the kind of teaching usually found in Hebrew schools. And they created a Confirmation ceremony to replace the Bar Mitzva ceremony at thirteen.

Naturally, the Orthodox rabbis objected to every change. But at that time, they were not a strong group. It was felt that the Reform movement might check the growing number of conversions to Christianity.

In Frankfurt am Main in Germany, in July 1845, the Conference of Rabbis of Germany stated;

"One of the marked achievements of the Reform movement has been the change in the status of women. This Conference declares that woman has the same obligations as man to participate from youth up in the instruction of Judaism and in the public services, and that the custom not to include women in the number of individuals necessary for the conducting of a public service is only a custom, and has no religious basis."

The following year the Breslau Conference granted women total equality. When Reform Judaism came to America, the 1892 Central Conference of American Rabbis adopted the following resolution:

"Whereas we have progressed beyond the idea of a secondary position of women in Jewish congregations, we recognize the importance of their hearty cooperation and active participation in congregational affairs; therefore be it resolved that women be eligible to full membership with all the privileges of voting and holding office in our congregation."

The first Reform-thinking Jews came to this country in the 1840s. Over the next twenty years, groups of Jews created "Reform Societies" which became Reform congregations, headed by German rabbis. In 1842, Har Sinai of Baltimore was the first congregation. Others were Emanuel of New York (1845) and Sinai of Chicago (1858).

Every move toward change was fought bitterly by Orthodox congregations. But from the beginning the Reform movement in Judaism changed the position of women.

In Reform congregations, women always sat with men, with their families, in a seating arrangement much more like the pews of a church than the divided areas of Orthodoxy.

Women were accepted as congregants equally with men. Women were called to the reading of the Torah from the beginning. Choirs singing during services had both men and women members.

The Reform movement was the first to train and ordain women rabbis and cantors. It has been in the forefront of discussions on women's rights and women's role in Judaism. Both boys and girls are honored at ceremonies to mark their coming of age at thirteen. And women take an active role in the running of the organization.

The Reform rabbinate has also been one of the first to recognize the growing number of interfaith marriages, and to rule that a child can take its Jewish heritage from either mother or father. Traditional Judaism says that a Jew is one born of a Jewish mother.

From a woman's perspective, Reform Judaism has taken giant steps toward reaching a state of equality in its practices.

Conservative

The American Conservative Jewish synagogues began in 1885, when Rabbi Sabato Morais and others formed the Jewish Theological Seminary Association in New York. The move began in anger against the lack of Jewish observance within the Reform movement. The incident which sparked the decision was a big banquet at which shrimp were served as the first course. (Shrimp are shellfish and "trefa," forbidden food.)

But the Conservative movement did not develop fully until the early 1900s, when Solomon Schechter was president of the Jewish Theological Seminary. He brought together sixteen communities to form the United Synagogue of America, designed to oppose the group of Reform synagogues, the Union of American Hebrew Congregations.

The Conservative Jews cling more to past tradition and observance, though recognizing some need for changes. Today, one of the largest denominations of American Jews allows Bat Mitzvas for girls. In some congregations women are called to the reading of the Torah, and may be counted as one of ten in a quorum or "minyan." In 1985, the first woman rabbi was ordained, and began work with her first congregation.

But there is great diversity among the attitudes in different Conservative communities, dependent on the attitude of the rabbi.

Reconstructionism

This small but interesting Jewish movement began in the 1920s, founded by Rabbi Mordechai M. Kaplan. Its origins were within the Conservative movement, but it later broke away.

Its perspective on Judaism is that of an evolving religious civilization of the Jewish people.

From the beginnings, its views on women were radically different from traditional viewpoints. Women were recognized as equals in all matters of personal status. The first Bat Mitzva ceremony was held by the Reconstructionist synagogue in the United States in 1922.

In 1951, women were called to read the Torah, and to be counted as part of the quorum or "minyan," and to perform any function in a synagogue service.

Women rabbis train at the Rabbinical College.

At the same time, the group also values many of the Jewish rituals, such as keeping a "kosher" home, and observing the holidays in a traditional Jewish style. And men and women are encouraged to learn Hebrew.

Orthodox

In the 1880s, Orthodox Jewish communities increased in America because of the wave of immigrants from Eastern Europe. By 1888, there were 130 Eastern European Orthodox synagogues in New York City.

Concern for their children's education led to the establishment of Orthodox schools. In 1887, a full-time elementary school, Ets-Chaim Talmudical Academy, was set up in New York. In 1896, the Rabbi Isaac Elchanan Theological Semi-

nary opened as the first "yeshivah," or Jewish study school, in
the country. Yeshivah University was established later.

In the early years of this century, many Orthodox families
left the community and joined Conservative synagogues.
However, in recent years, there's been renewed interest in
Orthodox observances, and a growing number of children
attend Orthodox Day Schools in New York City and the suburban areas.

From a woman's perspective, Orthodox Judaism is based
on the same laws of exclusion and discrimination which the
Hasidim follow. While different communities make decisions
as to how strictly the rules are followed, women sit separately
from men in services, separated by a high wall, a screen, a
curtain, a half screen, or a divider of some kind, or sit upstairs. They are not allowed to take part in the services. They
may not sing aloud, or in a synagogue choir. They may not
serve as rabbis or cantors. Girls do not have a religious ceremony of recognition at twelve or thirteen. Women have no
active role in synagogue observances.

The Orthodox like to propagate the myth that it is only the
devotees of the most devout aspects of the religion who de-
serve to survive, because they are keeping the true faith of
Judaism alive.

That's totally inaccurate, as one can learn from reading
any history of the Jews. Reform, Conservative, and even
unaffiliated Jews who survived the years of Jewish persecution can all bear living testimony to the true diversity of
Jewish thought and practice. Whoever has survived, and
whoever continues to practice the liberal, open-minded
and thinking beliefs of Judaism is keeping the true flame of
Judaic thought alive.

Many people, particularly women, who know little of the
history or the attitudes of Orthodoxy, feel inadequate if they
don't observe as much as they feel they should, or make an
ostentatious show of their beliefs, as the Orthodox do. They
harbor a simplistic fantasy that somewhere deep in the heart
of a devoutly Orthodox woman there is perfect harmony and
peace which the rest of us cannot find. That's the myth prop-
agated by Orthodox men. Women within Orthodoxy are

denied their rights, their individuality and the basic freedom and independence we take for granted.

There's a great deal more, and hundreds of books have been written on the subject, almost all of them by men. Throughout history, an occasional outstanding woman will appear, renowned for her knowledge or her abilities or her achievements. But she will always be kept from any role in the mainstream of Orthodoxy. She may found a women's organization as Henrietta Szold did when she created "Hadassah." She may agitate for women's rights as Ernestine Rose did, working with Susan B. Anthony in 1850 at the first national womens' rights convention at Worcester, Massachusetts, appearing as the featured speaker. She may choose the arena of politics and become prime minister of Israel, as Golda Meir did.

But within the confines of Orthodox practice, such women could have no effect. There are no women synagogue presidents, no women running synagogue organizations with men, and no organization for womens' rights recognized by the Orthodox community.

3

Childhood: The Perfect Time to Be Orthodox Because You Are Helpless and Everything Is Clear

To grow up inside the tight embrace of an Orthodox or Hasidic community is like growing up inside a carefully sealed hothouse. Everything thrives inside, but no one dares to venture out. After a while, the hot, steamy atmosphere begins to feel suffocating.

I don't remember very much of my early years. Soon after my birth, my parents moved to a house in the Orthodox community where they lived thereafter. When I was six, I started classes at the synagogue Hebrew school. I learned to read Hebrew, listened to stories about Biblical figures, and absorbed the reasons for the cycle of Jewish holidays.

Life for children is a rigid pattern of behavior, which provides a sense of security. There is the feeling that nothing will ever change and everything is exactly as it should be.

There are reasons for every prohibition ("You can't go to your grandma's today because it's the Sabbath and you can't take the bus") and explanations for even the most obscure of observances ("We dip the bitter herbs in salt water at Passover to remind us of the tears of the slaves in Egypt"). Children always like to have answers, and Orthodox beliefs provide them.

But even in those early years, boys are singled out for attention and girls begin to understand that life is not perfect. At the family Passover, there's a traditional order of events, including asking four questions about the celebration. The youngest son is supposed to ask the questions, but it's accepted that the youngest child may do so, even a daughter. However, in replying to the questions, the father recites an ancient parable about four sons and how they might ask these questions, reflecting different temperaments and interests. No matter how hard I looked through our lavishly illustrated "Haggadah," the prayer book for the Passover Service, I couldn't see a single little girl asking any questions at all.

Later on, in the Passover story, the Lord inflicts ten plagues on the Egyptians. The final and most terrible plague is striking dead the first-born sons. While I understood that killing children was cruel, the thought niggled at the back of my mind that killing first-born daughters might be just as wicked.

Why didn't anyone even mention what happened to the daughters in the story?

The answer, of course, is because those who wrote the books and retold the ancient stories were men, and had no interest in bolstering the egos of little girls. They knew that the Law favored boys and men. The thought of a different approach never crossed their minds.

From the Beginning

There really isn't a big difference between a one-day-old baby boy and a one-day-old baby girl. Wrapped in diapers, and a fancy white blanket, how can you tell them apart?

But in the male-dominated world of the Orthodox the differences are emphasized from the very first moment. A
woman gains status by giving birth to sons. She fails by having daughters.

One woman wrote about her birth in the 19th century:

"My arrival in this world was a disappointment to a number of people, and especially to my grandfather, Reb Chaim.
I was not a boy. . . . He hated me from the very first for the
disappointment and humiliation I had caused him."

A sociologist states that one of the events that shocks Jewish women into an awareness of equality is the birth of a
daughter, "when all the people who had planned to come to
the circumcision cancel their reservations."

And it's not unusual for community members to sympa-
thize with a father whose wife has borne him a daughter, and
wish him better luck next time.

Having children, however, is essential. Devout Orthodox
and Hasidic Jews do not recognize the 20th century development of safe methods of birth control. Some rabbis consider
that all couples should have at least two children, and once
they have performed that duty may ignore the lack of further offspring. Others assert that reproduction is unquestionably the decision of the Lord. In some cases, couples
even go to the rabbi to discuss whether or not to have more
children. Men and women don't feel they have the right to
take responsibility for childbearing. They need to hear the
advice of a rabbi before making that decision.

After all, the Bible is direct: "Be fruitful and multiply." In
order to modify that injunction, a woman has to take steps
to curb her childbearing, and most Orthodox and Hasidic
women are far too downtrodden to assert their own needs in
the face of religious dictates.

One woman read about a birth control device in a magazine, and without telling her husband, had one inserted so
that she would not have any more children. She did not feel
that she was causing him to disobey the injunction; she was
only a woman, so the action was not as sinful as if it had been
approved by a man.

Research studies show that of all groups, more Jewish

women use birth control methods, use them efficiently, and don't wait until after the birth of their first child to start using contraceptives. However, within Orthodoxy, there's a strange dichotomy: some rabbinic interpretations assert that women may use birth control only if the life of the mother is endangered, while others state that only wanted children should be brought into the world, so birth control is quite acceptable.

"There is a very real tension between the strictest position on birth control (even though it may be relatively permissive) and women's strong feelings about the sanctity of self-determination and their right to choose what happens to their own bodies," states Susan Weidman Schneider, in *Jewish and Female: Choices and Changes in our Lives Today.* "In fact, these laws and the conflicts they engender are a microcosm of the tensions between Judaism and feminism. Should some larger-than-life (male-dominated) system be permitted to create laws shaping women's lives?" No matter how sympathetic some liberal rabbis appear to be to the issue of birth control, "the implication for women . . . is the fact that these decision-makers have always been men," she says.

But there's no question at all about a woman's status in the community. She is supposed to be pregnant frequently. She is supposed to give birth to children as often as possible. And ideally, she should provide as many sons as she can.

In the eyes of the Hasidic and Orthodox community, the one moment when a woman reaches the pinnacle of perfection is when she gives birth to a baby boy. It's downhill all the way after that.

Having twin boys should be twice as good. But because Jewish law emphasizes the predominance of the first-born male, twins will only complicate the issue and lead to endless discussions on who was born first.

Having a girl is to move down into the second rank: first-born girls have no standing in Orthodox Judaism. They are no more important than any other girls; they're low on the totem pole.

Let's take a couple of average Orthodox Jewish families and see what happens when they have their first child, to show the steps along the way.

Avram and Ruth are newly married, just nine months. Avram works in his father-in-law's shoe store. Ruth was a secretary in the local Jewish school. Both of them were living at home with their parents, and both sets of parents are delighted with the marriage. Avram is 30, a little heavy, with a slight limp from a childhood car accident. Ruth has a bright smile, soft brown hair, and loves children.

Danny and Sarah have been married two years. Their strict upbringing left them in complete ignorance about how to consummate their marriage. It was only after Danny went to another community and had an examination with a doctor recommended by a friend that they found out what to do. Sarah became pregnant immediately, much to her relief.

Both women are Orthodox, and Ruth is Hasidically inclined, though not actively a member of the Hasidim. However, they both know they should not see a male doctor on their own, and prefer instead to go and talk to the rabbi.

When they do go to the doctor, their husbands accompany them, as is the case for most of their excursions outside the house.

During their months of pregnancy, it's unlikely that the rabbi will provide the women with details of childbirth preparation, exercises, diet and nutrition advice or extensive physical examinations. They will either muddle along in ignorance, hoping all is going well, or they will find a doctor and behave in a responsible modern fashion, sidestepping the rabbi's advice.

They will also have plenty of opportunity for gossip with other mothers, who will retell with relish the agonies of childbirth and what they suffered, and the terrible story of Hannah and have you heard what happened to Riva? In a tight ghetto community, the power of rumor and hearsay is multiplied a hundredfold. Ruth and Sarah will be suitably apprehensive about the myriad disasters which might strike. They are unlikely to find a group of women from a variety of backgrounds to share experiences. And a birth preparation course offered by a non-religious organization or a local hospital is out of the question.

Then there are the superstitions and old wives' tales. Lilith figures prominently in many of them.

Lilith is a woman thrown out of the Garden of Eden because she wanted to be Adam's equal, according to the myths. In the first chapter of Genesis, woman is created as man's equal. But in the second chapter, she is created out of his ribs.

These two versions have inspired countless folk tales to explain the discrepancy. One suggests that Lilith, like Adam, was created out of the earth. But because they were of the same origin, she refused to obey him. In a quarrel, she flew away from him and refused to return, despite the intercession of a vanguard of three heavenly angels.

In the end her life was spared in exchange for one concession. In the future, she would always harm babies. Until the eighth day after their birth she could injure boys, and until the twentieth day of their birth, she could injure girls. But she agreed that if she saw the names of three angels written in the home, she would keep away from the child.

So today, during childbirth, women often have amulets or signs hung in the room with the names of three angels. Or they shout the names aloud. Or even sound the Shofar, the ram's horn, which would certainly divert a mother in labor, if nothing else. And in the first days after the birth, some people use a false name for the child, to distract the evil spirits like Lilith. And keep watch the night before the circumcision to guard the child. Ruth and Sarah probably follow many of these ancient superstitions, just to be on the safe side.

It's a sad reflection on the warped rabbinic interpretation of a woman's psychology that he automatically assumes that women would harm children. In all the history of the family, it is the woman who has cared for and nurtured the children, and given them education. It is the woman who has unselfishly given of her time and energy to focus on her family. And it is women who are ordained by Jewish law to raise children.

Yet the rabbis have twisted the reality to show that an independent woman like Lilith is wicked and dangerous. She must be feared. She must be guarded against. And other women must learn to avoid them.

The rabbis prefer to promote the image of Eve, devout and submissive, taken from Adam's rib, and fearful of her male companion. They emphasize the dutiful role of the long-suffering Biblical wives like Sarah and Rebecca, Leah and Rachel. And they encourage the superstitious fear of Lilith as a way of showing the dangers of women wanting equality.

Baby Boy = Good: Baby Girl = Bad

One day, two tiny babies are born.

For Avram and Ruth, it's their first child. It's a boy! Joy is unconfined. The news is phoned from relative to relative. It's a boy! The first child is a boy!

For newborn Sammy, the attention in the first few weeks may prove to be a little painful. But right now, his face is pink and shiny, and his eyes are shut. He has fulfilled every dream of doting parents, grandparents, relatives, friends and religious leaders.

Social success in religious communities is marked by having children. Jewish parents, in-laws, friends and even casual acquaintances don't hesitate to ask couples: "Been married long? A year? Well? How many children?"

Now that Sammy has arrived, an enormous burden has been lifted from Avram and Ruth's shoulders. They have finally made it as acceptable Jews. And they have a son. A son!

Over at Danny and Sarah's house, things are a little less rosy. Yes, it's their first child. Yes, the baby's fine and the mother is fine. But it's—it's—it's a girl. Yes, it's a girl. What a shame!

Sarah knows that despite her joy in her daughter, and Danny's interest in their new baby, she has failed. Her role is to produce sons. Even Danny says to her, "Well, next time we'll have a son."

They call her Deborah, after Danny's late grandmother.

Ruth and Avram are elated about their firstborn son. So are their parents. Sammy's neck is a little wobbly, and his eyes find it hard to focus. You have to hold him carefully, and keep your hand firmly under his head. He has tiny, perfectly formed fingers and little pink toes. He waves his two crinkly soft feet in the air. He cries. He gurgles. He sucks noisily.

If you've not held a week-old baby in a while, try to imagine what it's like. This tiny bundle of humanity who has been alive for such a short time begs for love and care and attention. He's happy when he's fed. He's contented when he's dry and warm. He falls asleep while they're drilling a hole outside in the road, and stays awake crying in the still of the night.

However, if you are an Orthodox Jew, the only thing you really worry about is his penis. Why? Because as soon as he's made it through the first seven days, you are going to invite a crowd of friends over, serve food and drink, and have your basic-black-bearded rabbi, expert in slicing and called a "Mohel," come over and chop a piece off Sammy's penis.

That's the rule according to the Code of Jewish Law. The behavior is set down clearly. This is no time to find a qualified doctor, and have the operation in a germ-free environment. Nope. It's always been done in a crowded room, lots of people, plenty of noise, and one howling baby.

The baby's preferences are not taken into account. Most babies like quiet, painless days, while someone comforting and predictable looks after them. In all my dealings with babies, I have not found one who enjoyed being sliced, stabbed or pricked by sharp instruments, particularly not on the penis.

But Orthodox Judaism is not interested in human feelings or the emotional reactions of a tiny baby. If the ancient laws demand that baby boys have their foreskins sliced off by rabbis, that's what will be done.

I once attended a circumcision. I have never forgotten the experience. I was twenty-one and visiting Israel. One weekend we went to a religious "kibbutz," a collective farm.

On the Sunday morning, a circumcision ceremony took place in the main meeting hall. We all filed in, chatting and laughing.

When the room was almost full, the family came in, and

walked up to the platform. There were about a dozen people, mostly men, including a black-robed rabbi. They crowded round so that we could only see their backs. We glimpsed the tiny baby on a table in the middle. There was the mumbling of prayers and chanting. The rabbi swayed.

Suddenly there was a piercing scream of pain from the baby, followed by cries of anguish and howling terror. Then there was agonized sobbing and crying. The people in the hall clapped and shouted "Mazeltov!" meaning "Good luck!" and the talking and laughing continued, drowning out the screams of the baby. The ceremony ended. Wine and cake were served. Everyone congratulated the parents and relatives.

In the context of modern Israel, the ceremony was like having a bowl of icy water thrown in your face. Here was a thriving new Jewish society. And yet here was an ancient ceremony being conducted with the same voyeuristic liplicking delight with which people must have watched public hangings, whippings, executions.

A crowd of modern, adult people stood cheering on a man with a knife who sliced the penis of a tiny baby, causing great pain and discomfort for no good reason other than "Tradition."

Most Jews do choose to have their sons circumcised. But there's a difference between a quiet, private event carried out by a surgeon or qualified medical practitioner, with perhaps a local anesthetic, in peaceful surroundings; and the repulsiveness of a public circus, with men and women praising an act of violence.

The reason Orthodox Judaism bans mothers from an active part in the ceremony is that if they had had a role in the official slicing, one or two of them might have protested.

There are also serious medical questions raised today about the benefits of circumcision. A recent statement of the American Academy of Pediatrics notes:

"A program of education leading to continuing good personal hygiene would offer all the advantages of routine circumcision without the attendant surgical risk," and adds: "The foreskin protects the glans throughout life."

The American College of Obstetricians and Gynecologists and the American Pediatric Urologic Society both agree that circumcision is not essential for total health care.

In a health column in *The New York Times* in 1985, Jane E. Brody outlined some of the problems of circumcising babies. One in 500 cases has significant ill effects, including serious bleeding and infection, she notes.

"There have been occasional disastrous mishaps, including excessive cutting of penile tissue, severe infection or gangrene that resulted in loss of the penis and even death," she writes.

Without the foreskin, the glans is exposed to constant irritation by diapers in infancy, and by clothing and other substances later, she says. Further, there is clearly *no* proof that the operation prevents premature ejaculation in adults. Physicians who have studied the risks and benefits urge parents to be well-informed beforehand, and to have the circumcision done only by "well-trained physicians using careful surgical techniques," she emphasizes.

Even the rabbis writing in the distant Biblical past knew that circumcision is a life-threatening danger for a small baby boy. The Code of Jewish Law includes the following comments:

> "If a woman has lost two sons from the effect of circumcision, her third son should not be circumcised until he gets older and stronger. If a woman has lost a child because of the circumcision, and the same thing happened to her sister's son, then the children of the other sisters should not be circumcised until they grow older and stronger."

Once again, we're looking at laws which were made hundreds of years before modern understanding about antiseptics and germs, before easily accessible pure water and simple anesthetics.

But the rigidity of Orthodox thinking has no mechanism for adapting to discoveries which were never dreamed of in Biblical and Talmudic times. Instead, they simply continue with practices which fly in the face of rational behavior, and perpetuate traditions which at best are foolish and at worst disastrous.

The Redemption of the Firstborn: Boys Only, of Course

Let's assume that Sammy is one of the lucky babies who survives the anguish of his circumcision. His birth will be marked by another significant religious ceremony, a second reminder for his parents that it's better to have a boy.

"The Redemption of the Firstborn" is an ancient custom dating back to the times when the Temple stood in Jerusalem, more than 2,000 years ago. In those days, it was the custom to consecrate the firstborn son to service in the Temple and to give him to the priests at a suitable age, to fulfill the Temple duties.

However, as the years went by, the customs changed. The Jews living in Israel were divided up into twelve tribes, and the descendants of the tribe of Levi took over the duties of Temple services. From that change, a tradition emerged in which parents would redeem their firstborn from Temple service by paying money to a member of another tribe, the Cohens.

Today, since the Temple no longer exists, the ceremony is a ritual redemption. It takes place at least thirty days after the child's birth. As usual, it's an all-male event. The father and the baby boy meet with a Cohen, descendants of that tribe, usually in the parents' home. The father says he will redeem his son from Temple service, and pays the equivalent of five pieces of silver.

The father says: "I desire to redeem my son, and here thou has the value of his redemption, which I am bound to give according to the Torah"

The Cohen then pronounces two blessings, and says, holding the money over the head of the child:

"This is instead of that, this in commutation for that, this in remission of that. May this child enter into life, into the Torah, and the fear of Heaven. May it be God's will that even as he has been admitted to redemption, so may he enter into the Torah, the nuptial canopy, and into good deeds. Amen."

Then he gives a traditional blessing, and it's over.

Usually there's a small party to celebrate the event, for which the women may prepare the food. They are not allowed to take part in any of the proceedings.

Meanwhile, how is little Debbie doing after her first week on this earth?

Well, she's happily gurgling at home. The community isn't too interested in her. A month after her birth, during a Sabbath service, her father is called up to read from the scrolls, as an honor. He announces the name of his daughter.

The mother as always is completely ignored.

There are no official religious ceremonies of any kind to welcome a newborn girl into the Jewish community of Orthodoxy. The Biblical law of succession is crystal clear: the son always comes before the daughter.

There's no circumcision ceremony, of course. And no Redemption of the Firstborn, even if she is a firstborn. After all, she's only a girl.

Some ardent feminists, eager to reconcile the madness of Orthodoxy's attitudes toward women and their own desire to be part of this extremist community, have suggested that perhaps a ceremony where a baby girl's hymen is ruptured could be instituted to match the ceremony of circumcision.

That's the kind of bizarre thinking that develops when you've been reading Talmudic rules and discussions for too long.

It's bad enough that a week-old baby boy is sliced apart in front of a mob of adults with little concern for his health. Why double the pain by inflicting vicious surgery on innocent week-old baby girls? Why should they be made to scream desperately too?

Far better to leave the decision about penis-slicing to parents and the privacy of medical deliberations.

Some couples are creating new ceremonies to mark the arrival of baby daughters. A group of women rabbis suggest a ritual washing of the feet of newborn girls, which they call Brit Rechitza. Another couple dunked their daughter in a miniature bath, reflecting the role of the "Mikveh" or ritual bath in women's lives. And a collection of seven welcoming ceremonies for Jewish girls is available from the Ezrat Nashim, a Jewish feminist organization meaning "Help of Women," within Conservative Judaism.

Such ceremonies mark the birth of a daughter and have importance far beyond the actual occasion. One mother admits:

"I count myself among those shamefaced parents of ten-year-old girls who must explain to them that, no, there are no pictures of a family party at the time of her birth (as there are for her brother) because she was named in a synagogue, one weekday morning when her father was called to the Torah, and the [mostly male] early morning "daveners" [people praying] shared a bottle of schnapps and that was that."

Many new ceremonies are being created, and the Jewish Women's Resource Center in New York keeps an informal collection of them.

None of these have been recognized by Orthodox or Hasidic communities.

My Own Early Childhood

Friends often say, when I describe the life of Orthodox children, "Well, you managed pretty well, so it can't have been that bad."

My experience was interrupted. When I was about two and a half years old the Second World War erupted. We lived in London, and the Government ruled that all young children should be evacuated. My parents decided to send me to Canada with my grandmother. So I set off with her.

She was my mother's mother, a widow, in her sixties. She and her husband had come from Poland in the early 1900s, and made new lives for themselves and their five children in England. They bought property, went into the marble importing business, and saw their children grow up and marry. One son became a docttor.

My grandmother was a feisty, independent woman who never pretended to feel any empathy with Orthodox Judaism. Her own brand was minimal, and individualist. For almost four of my most formative years, until I was six years old, I lived with her. She always told me, "You can do anything you want to do, anything." She encouraged me to go sledding, took me to the beach, enrolled me in kindergarten, bandaged my cut knees and showed me that a woman can cope beautifully on her own, in a strange country, with few resources. It was a very different message from the one I would have received from my parents.

When I returned as a lively six-year-old, I was suddenly enveloped in a tight, Orthodox Jewish community where girls were second-class citizens. My parents' lives revolved around their Orthodox beliefs, which now I was expected to accept.

"Don't touch that! You can't write on the Sabbath!"

"Don't put that spoon there! It's a milk spoon, and that's a meat drawer!"

The laws of keeping a "kosher" home demand the complete separation of all meat and milk dishes and cutlery.

"Don't do that! Get dressed for the synagogue now or we'll be late."

As a parent, I know that saying "No" and "Don't" take up inordinate amounts of time. But as an Orthodox parent, there are twice as many regulations. You have to teach children not to touch a hot stove, and not to put the dishes in the wrong place. You encourage them to read and write, but explain that some things are forbidden on the Sabbath and holidays. And you have to teach them what they can eat and what they must never touch, designed to instill them with a sense of guilt about whatever they put in their mouths.

The basic duty of the Orthodox parent is to create a permanent sense of guilt in their children.

Perhaps they find a coin in the pocket of the coat they are wearing on the Sabbath, and agonize over whether it is worse to take the coin out and thus touch money on the Sabbath, or leave it there and have to carry it around all day.

Perhaps they read the wrong prayer from the prayerbook during the service and miss the special prayer for the New Moon.

Perhaps they start thinking the wrong thoughts in the bathroom and then feel terrible for what they thought.

The Orthodox system is designed to provide maximum insecurity and discomfort for young children in exchange for the blanket-warmth of acceptance within the community. It's a powerful mixture.

I read an account of a young woman who was "love-bombed" by a cult group. For days she received unstinting love and affection and was told exactly what to do to be accepted. When she did it, she was wholeheartedly welcomed into the group, and thrilled to be one of its members. Yet, at the same time, she could see that much of what she was doing was foolish, unacceptable and not what she had ever wanted to do before.

Orthodox Judaism has the same effect. It explains exactly what you have to do, and when you do it, assures you that you are doing everything right and all is well. You are a good Jew. The problems come if you start to think about what you are doing.

My parents weren't Hasidim, but took a more modern Orthodox approach. While we observed strict rules in some areas, I wore clothes that were acceptable in the society in which we lived. I wore a uniform to school. On weekends I wore more casual clothes. And for going to the synagogue I wore special clothes, and of course a hat. How I hated wearing hats! But in my community, a simple headscarf was not enough. It had to be a fashionable hat, which matched whatever else you wore, and looked right.

I attended the local synagogue Hebrew school, with boys, from the age of about seven. There I learned Hebrew, and the stories of the Jewish festivals, the history of the Jews, the prayers and blessings, and the slow realization that no matter how well I studied, and no matter how hard I tried, even the most foolish boy in the class would be able to be called to the Reading of the Law before I could be considered.

"She should have been a boy!" said a well-meaning friend of my parents on hearing how well I had done at the Hebrew school. It was a devastating moment. Why had I not been a boy, I wondered? What was so awful and wrong about being a girl? Was there nothing I could do about it? Little girls were supposed to be beautiful. No one ever said that to me. Little girls were supposed to be good, and I didn't seem to be very good. And now just because I had won a prize for my studying, it wasn't really significant because I was a girl. There was a deep sense of having failed, and of never being able to correct the error.

The Hebrew school also emphasized that there were Good Jews, who observed more of the picayune details than anyone else, and the Bad Jews, who broke some of the rules.

Every Sunday morning, the principal of the school at the weekly assembly lectured us about religious behavior.

"There are those of you whose parents ride on the Sabbath, don't keep a kosher home, and don't observe the rules we must all keep," he would say, his round face reddening and his rimless glasses steaming up. "That is not good enough. We teach you how to behave, we teach you what to observe, and you must go home and tell your parents what they are doing wrong. You have a responsibility to tell them what you have learned and lead them in the proper paths."

He'd go on for about ten minutes or so while we stood shuffling our feet and nudging and whispering to each other. Sometimes he would bring in a specific example of having seen someone actually getting on a bus on a Jewish festival day, or noticed some of the students going into the non-kosher restaurant in our community. He would urge us to tell our fellow students to observe the laws and behave as Good Jews. We were responsible for all our fellow Jews, he'd say.

The idea sounded downright unpleasant to me. Why was it any business of his or ours how observant people were? I always think of the comment of an old man we knew on Cape Cod, who said, whenever he saw a Hasidic Jew, "Here come the Thought Police."

Superstition and Fears

Like primitive people, Orthodox and Hasidic parents are steeped in superstition. They are forever warding off the Evil Eye, or avoiding dangerous spirits, or trying to protect

themselves from unseen evil, or hastily insuring a project by
invoking God's blessing, in conversation or in writing.

I once read a wonderful letter, typical of this approach,
which included sentences like:

"I'm glad to tell you that Mimi came round with her two
little girls, both well, K.H., and they plan to visit her mother
next week, P.G., who is not out of the hospital and recov-
ering slowly T.G."

It's customary to use initials like this for invoking good
spirits. They represent old Yiddish phrases meaning:

K.H. = Ke-ayin Hora, may we avoid the Evil Eye;
P.G. = Please God, may it be all right;
T.G. = Thank God, may we be grateful it was all right.

The ultra devout write them in Hebrew or Yiddish letters,
so that a page may be filled with the strange squiggles of invocations among the lines, like an undertone to ward off evil
possibilities at every turn.

Letters from my parents were usually confined to the P.G.,
and T.G. options, since they didn't know much Yiddish. And
I've even seen B.H. used, which stands for the Hebrew words
"Baruch Hashem" or "Blessed be the Name," instead of T.G.

Children absorb these superstitious fears from the earliest
years. There's a belief that Evil Spirits like to capture the
souls of little boys. So the Orthodox avoid cutting the hair of
little boys until they are three years old. That way, the Evil
Spirits won't be able to tell who are the little boys and who are
the little girls.

Everyone knows that the Evil Spirits are not in the least interested in the souls of little girls. It's the reason the extreme
Orthodox and Hasidim let their little sons run around with
long untidy curls for the first few years. And the first haircut,
at the age of three, has become another ceremony of significance for the boys whose parents observe this custom.

Sammy's parents also allow his long sidecurls to grow.
This, too, is based on an obscure Biblical rule which has been
given extraordinary emphasis and importance. From all I
have learned of hairstyles in the days of the prophets, long

sidecurls were not in vogue. But the style had been established in the ghettoes of Europe in the Middle Ages, and it's now de rigueur among the ultra-Orthodox today.

For the girls, the rules are repressive, not expressive. The rabbis, in their malicious distaste for women, were mostly concerned that women be dressed modestly.

According to the English translation of *A Woman's Guide to Jewish Observance,* which brings together many of the laws relating to Orthodox observances for women, "it is a serious transgression for a woman to dress immodestly."

Jewish law requires that women have to cover:

a) the neck, below and including the collarbone (with a special note emphasizing that the area above the collarbone may be exposed);
b) the arms, the upper arms, including the elbow (with a special note that a woman may not weave in the marketplace because she will invariably expose her arm in public);
c) the legs, the thighs, including the knees.

The laws then go into great detail about how a woman must wear a dress or skirt which is long enough to cover her knees "whether she is standing or sitting, and this is necessary even if she wears non-transparent stockings."

One school of thought feels ankle-length dresses are essential, but that view did not prevail.

But the stockings are important. There's a rule that a woman should wear stockings at home "because strangers or visitors may come at any time." One noted rabbi says that a man may not say his prayers or study the Torah if his wife is not wearing stockings in communities where it is the accepted practice to wear them.

However, don't think that women are given the same consideration! A devout woman, dutifully following the rules may recite her prayers "in the presence of a man, even if normally-covered parts of his body are exposed." So he can strip down and parade around while she can't complain. And he can call her a sinner if she takes off her stockings.

These modesty laws apply to girls from their earliest years. A girl under six is allowed to wear short skirts "if she wears socks or tights that cover the rest of her legs. Even if the child wears a long skirt, it is still proper for her to wear socks or tights."

However, she can't come to the synagogue in her short skirt, even if she is wearing tights, because she would be so immodest that men could pray in her presence. "A girl should be dressed modestly in public beginning at age three," asserts the rabbinic regulations.

There are no laws demanding modesty from little boys, preventing them from exposing their knobby knees or letting a collar slip from their scrawny necks. There aren't any stipulations about them wearing long tights or skirts to cover their immodest genitalia. They could even bare their forearms and weave in the marketplace if they felt like it.

It seems to me that the rabbis thought little boys were perfectly fine, and had no need to consider offending women. But they immediately spotted all kinds of dreadful offensive possibilities in little girls, which rabbis over the centuries have determinedly embellished.

Children brought up with this warped attitude toward bare skin, modest dress and the feeling that bodies are dirty and dangerous and must be hidden, absorb an extremely biased view of people outside who don't conform to these rigid rules.

For a year, I lived in Jerusalem. I shared a cramped apartment with two Israeli women and an English woman. We had the first floor of a white-painted house, situated on a narrow winding alleyway near the section called "Mea She'arim." This is still the area where many Hasidic and extreme Orthodox families live, with many small synagogues and religious schools.

The two Israelis studied at the university, and the English woman worked as a statistician. I found a job as a typist.

One hot summer afternoon, I was walking back from work. I watched two little girls skipping along toward me. They both wore the long sleeves, the drooping skirts and the thick stockings of children brought up within the Orthodox community. I was wearing a summer skirt and shirt, and sandals.

As they came past me, they shouted vindictively:

"Protsa! Protsa!" which means "Prostitute!" They didn't stop to discuss the matter, since in their hearts they already presumed they were right.

I was shocked. But I wondered about their education. Did they believe that anyone not wearing the long sleeves, the thick stockings and the long skirts was a prostitute?

Was that how they saw the hundreds of women walking around? Had they already been taught that young women must never go out alone without a man? Had they already been indoctrinated into the beliefs of helplessness? Had they already learned that they were unable to do anything on their own, and certainly could not walk around the city in modern summer clothes? Did they already hate all those who would not conform to their behavior? And what did they do with their own feelings, their emotions, their desires as they grew into adolescence and adulthood?

I often watched the families of the ultra-religious community who lived along the cobbled streets in the picturesque area near the market. The men wore the thick heavy black garments and hats which might have been comfortable in the cool breezes of Poland but were strangely oppressive in the blazing white light of Jerusalem.

The women always walked alongside, demurely. Or they followed behind. Or they pushed the baby carriage. There were always children. Sometimes they ran alongside their parents, sometimes they walked, sometimes they sat and were pushed. The boys had the long hair and the curls; the girls wore scarves round their heads, longsleeved blouses, skirts to their knees, white stockings, heavy shoes.

Perhaps at home they laughed and played together. Perhaps away from the cobbled streets they untied their heavy shoes and loosened their clothes, and relaxed. But it was hard to believe.

Their world had already been divided into two camps: those who were good and observed all the rules of Orthodox behavior; and those wicked prostitutes and immoral women outside who showed their bare arms.

The Dividing Moment

In the writings by Jewish women about life within an Orthodox community, there's often a moment when the sudden realization of unfair discrimination becomes crystal clear.

For me that happened when I was ten years old. Every year, the five books of the Torah are read aloud in the synagogue. At the conclusion of the readings, there's a festival called "The Rejoicing of the Law" or "Simhat Torah." That evening, dancing, singing and unruly celebrations take place in the synagogue to mark the joyous occasion of completing the scrolls.

It's a time when children march in procession in the synagogue behind the men, and wave flags and sing. Often candies and cakes are distributed, and the atmosphere is alive with exuberant excitement.

For all the children it's a wonderful evening to play and have fun. It was hilarious to see the minister and the serious leaders of the community behaving as irresponsibly as the children, dancing around with the scrolls amid the noise.

But that year, my father said to me as I talked about the evening, "You are too old to come downstairs. You must sit with your mother."

I was appalled, but he was adamant.

"You are too old to come downstairs. You won't be admitted."

I can still feel the sense of isolation and pain at missing out on the fun, as I sat upstairs in the Ladies Balcony, looking down on the men and boys and little girls enjoying themselves, laughing, dancing and singing.

My mother had little sympathy. "It's about time you started to behave properly," she said. "You can watch everything that's happening. What's the difference?"

But I knew there was a difference. For reasons which had nothing to do with my devotion, my abilities as a Hebrew student, my observances of the multitude of Jewish laws, I had been deprived of taking part in a celebration which I loved. I felt a deep sense of injustice as I watched my brother and his friends enjoying themselves. And for the first time I understood that there was something wrong with me in the eyes of Judaism, and nothing I could do would be able to make it right.

4

Education: What Is Happening in Orthodox and Hasidic Schools and What Children Are Learning

The Jewish tradition reveres book learning and study. But it is usually reserved for men. Women stay home to look after the house or earn money while the men go off to learn with the other men at distant seminaries.

There's an often-quoted story about the famous scholar, Rashi, which was told to me as an example of how women should behave.

Rashi left his wife and went away for twenty-four years, it's said, to study. When he returned home, surrounded by admirers, his wife came out to meet him. He halted the procession to acknowledge her and said, "Here is the woman who has made it all possible." That was the ideal role for a woman: to provide support and devotion for her husband's learning.

One learned rabbi has said, "Whoever teaches his daughter Torah, teaches her lasciviousness."

It simply wasn't acceptable for girls or women to study the Bible and its interpretations, in the past.

But Jewish communities adjust in some ways to the influences of the society in which they live. The United States offers free education to all children. The Orthodox, much as they dislike the concept, now accept the idea of educating girls as well as boys. There are Hasidic and Orthodox schools for both sexes, where religious studies are emphasized.

The trouble with any religion-based education is that it's sadly out of date, and there's very little anyone can do about it.

Comparing religious education and secular education is like looking at one tree, which has grown to its full height and only repeats the annual cycle of shedding and growing its leaves, and an ever-expanding forest of trees, where new stalks are continually sprouting and older trees are constantly developing.

We happen to be living in an age of technological development. The Bible doesn't cover technology. You can't find out how to build a car or discover penicillin by studying the Bible, no matter how assiduously. You'll never learn how to use a word processor or ride a bicycle either. And you'll never find out about electricity or solar heat or nuclear power by analysing the tractates.

What's more, in this century, women's lives have changed, so their experiences are quite different from the ones described in the Bible.

Women in America don't go to the well to draw water. They don't weave cloth for their garments. They certainly don't herd sheep in the cities where most Orthodox Jews live.

The tragedy of the Hasidic and Orthodox school systems, and of the Bible-based schools of other denominations, is that the foundation on which they're standing is cracked and doomed to collapse. But they keep pretending nothing's wrong.

Some religious schools valiantly encourage their students to follow a secular education to the best of their abilities. But the danger is clear: once a thoughtful student begins to examine the assertions of Biblical belief against the realities of today's world, it's hard to reconcile the two.

Most religious schools prefer to be safe, rather than secular. They teach a limited course of study of those topics which they consider controversial, and they eliminate those they'd rather not know about.

Instead, they emphasize the benefits of devotion to a religious life in contrast to "Those Out There" who have no devout faith.

This pattern is clear in Hasidic and extreme Orthodox schools, as it is in extreme Catholic and fundamentalist Protestant schools. If teachers don't want to discuss how babies are born, why some people are homosexual, and whether women can be President, they will carefully avoid those topics.

It's not that children don't learn anything. They don't learn enough about what will help them cope in the world of today. Instead they are prepared for a closed, narrow world where fear of the outside looms large.

Once you're in the real world, you take so much for granted that you forget how much those in the ghetto are missing.

Girls in the real world see women working in a variety of positions. They see women police officers directing traffic. They see women driving buses. They see television news stories about women at political events. They see mothers of their friends working. They see women jogging around the streets or playing tennis.

Children learn from everything they see. But little girls cut off inside the ultra-Orthodox ghetto perceive a strangely biased view of life. They see only men in positions of authority. They see women at home, overworked mothers and housekeepers. If they have women teachers, they must wonder how such women can work and look after their children. They never see women exercising or women asserting themselves or women in positions of authority in the world outside.

Nor is praise ever given to a woman for achieving distinction. There's only condemnation for women who try to do more than what is expected of them. Women should be demure, be quiet and be at home, is the message. And, as many of us know who remember those repressivè messages of the past, it's hard to fight the tide of negativism about what women can do.

What's Going On in the Hasidic Schools?

It's not easy to find out what is happening inside the Hasidic world, or in its schools. There's an aura of secrecy and insularity which is hard to penetrate. And, like religious schools of every denomination, there's no demand for accountability to an outside authority.

New York's Jewish schools file details of their curricula with the Board of Jewish Education in New York City. Here statistics and information are compiled and prepared for those who wish to find out what is being taught.

"We don't know what the Hasidic schools are teaching nor some of the more extreme Orthodox schools because they don't give us their curricula," said one staff member. "They don't even share them with each other, so that each school is entirely individual in what it decides to teach."

Some schools, it's known, have only two hours a day of secular subjects and spend the rest of the time on religious and Hebrew studies. Others spend more time on secular topics. Some include swimming as a sports activity. Some separate boys and girls from the start, while others allow them to study together until the high school level.

I decided to try to visit a Hasidic school. A friend gave me the name of one, and I called to ask permission. After numerous phone calls to the secretary, I spoke briefly to an assistant principal. She was too busy to consider my visiting the school. She was unable to talk on the telephone. There was no one else I could talk to. It was clear that she didn't want to discuss curriculum details with an outsider.

I called another school, this time asking only that they send me a brochure or any printed materials they might give out, so that I could have some idea of what they taught.

"How old are your children?" the woman asked.

"This isn't for my children," I explained.

I heard her talking to someone in the background.

"Well, I can't talk to you about it," she said. I gave her my name and address. But nothing came in the mail.

Perhaps they were just busy. Perhaps I sounded suspicious, though I've called for information from schools, from government offices, from businesses and from individuals many, many times, mostly quite successfully. I know when people don't want to talk to me, and I usually accept their right to remain silent.

I considered dressing up as a Hasidic mother and going to see a school. But somehow it felt wrong. Why were they so afraid to give me information?

The Hasidim in this country belong to one of two groups, the Satmars or the Lubavitchers. They are bitterly divided, and each group runs its own schools and high schools.

Some secular subjects are taught, to both boys and girls. But modern biology is never taught to either sex. All teachings related to science and the theory of evolution are ignored. Nothing is taught that conflicts with Biblical beliefs.

Like the fundamentalist Christian schools, they don't like their students to absorb any education that might cause them to doubt their religious teachings. This isn't the place to find a discussion group on women's rights. The major emphasis is on religious education.

The message at every stage for the girls is to urge them forward to marry and have children. Their roles are clearly defined, no matter what their interests at school. And they, like the boys, study a great deal of the Bible, the commentaries and the observances necessary.

It's interesting to note that even women who have come into the Hasidic movement from the outside world, and keep their ties to professional careers, send their daughters to be brought up denied of any opportunities. It's as if they want to deprive them of choice instead of striving to help them succeed in their adult lives.

Although the Hasidim emphasize that girls can only turn

into perfect wives and mothers, there's no recognition that there have been great strides in understanding those roles.

Educated women today study nutritional information, read texts on child development, analyze the best ways to run a household, and recognize the need for careful budgeting. The specialty of Home Economics has moved a long way from the old days of learning to make toast and sew clothes. There's a tremendous amount of research available which relates to the work of keeping house, preparing meals and taking care of children, and family.

If the Hasidim really wanted to prepare the young girls of their community for their home-bound roles, they could bring in chefs and cooks to teach them how to improve the cuisine of the super-kosher kitchen. They could invite child psychiatrists to teach courses on child development and parental roles. They could teach basic accounting, so that girls would know how to budget for their families. And they could present courses by professional housecleaners on the best way to take care of furniture and fittings.

But they don't really want women to have much knowledge. They just want to see them doing the things their mothers and grandmothers did.

The teachers in the schools are also bound to teach from the perspective in which the school is rooted. This is not the place for individuality or personal development. It's a training ground for total conformity.

I mentioned to an Orthodox friend that I'd had a difficult time finding out what goes on in the schools.

She laughed.

"Look," she said, "if you're an Orthodox parent and you decide to send your child to an Orthodox or Hasidic school, you know what they are teaching. That's why you chose it in the first place. You know they are going to teach from a strictly Orthodox point of view, that the emphasis will be on religious subjects, and that traditional attitudes will prevail. If you have to ask, they know you're not Orthodox."

She was right.

If I had wanted to send my daughter to an Orthodox school, I would already be convinced that her place was at

home, and that only marriage and motherhood could ever
bring her satisfaction.

I'd be delighted that she spent half the day in religious
studies, analyzing the ancient laws about keeping the Sabbath and not eating pork.

I'd be perfectly happy for her to meet only children from
identical Orthodox Jewish backgrounds.

But because I'm not that kind of parent, I sent both my
children to public schools, where they succeeded admirably
by my standards.

I'm absolutely certain that the most important step a parent of a daughter can take is to make sure that she has a solid,
extensive education. That was always important, but today it
is essential.

Why? Because we are living through a time when women
can take unlimited opportunities, and when their lives are
changing so rapidly that it's hard to see what lies ahead. We
are experiencing social revolution, and it has only just begun.

The Century of Women

The concept seems dramatic. But if you look around at the
evidence, the pieces fall into place. Throughout the world,
the changes in technology, chemistry, biology and behavior
have affected women more than any other group.

And these changes, unlike the occasional breakthroughs of
the past which benefited a few educated or wealthy women,
influence the lives of women in every class, of every religion
and of every nationality.

From the beginning of the 20th century, women have
moved forward from helplessness, uneducated, weak de-
pendents to strong, independent, healthy people.

Little of the excitement of new opportunities percolates
down to the little girls growing up in the Hasidic or extreme
Orthodox communities. Perhaps they hear a few rumors of
some achievements by women. Perhaps they learn of women
who succeeded in politics or sports. But they are excluded
from those opportunities.

The most depressing aspect of the narrow-minded teachings of extreme Judaism is that it deprives the growing generation of girls from finding any place for themselves in the world of tomorrow. In the past, women's lives were not that different from the lives of the women now living within the ghetto of the Hasidim or the extreme Orthodox communities. They had no education, no birth control, no political rights, no training for a career, no way of finding economic independence. Today, the revolution has begun. Women are experiencing a century of dramatic change in every aspect of their lives. It may be difficult to accept some of the changes. It may be hard to adjust to new patterns of behavior. And it's always unsettling when long-held beliefs and traditions are pushed aside.

But the changes are here. They are real. They are visible.

The rabbis and leaders of extremist groups would like to bury their heads in the sands of history and deny that anything is different. They want the girls of today to learn exactly what they learned forty years ago. They want them to grow up exactly like the women of the past.

They remind me of the slave-owners of the 18th century who insisted that the world would collapse if slavery ended. They assured everyone that the slaves were happy in captivity, and didn't want to be free. And they insisted that no good would come of ending a long tradition. They would stand with their slaves assuring the world, "See how happy they are!" And the slaves, knowing there were no choices, would nod and smile obligingly.

Just as the wives of the Hasidic community do today.

It's That Old Time Learning

Romanticists like to believe that's there something intrinsically good about the system of education which Orthodox Judaism has developed. I know that it's successful in one way: it turns out people who know how to parrot what they have been taught. But it's quite useless for coping with the reality of life in our world.

When children start learning how to read the Torah in Hebrew and translate, they don't begin with the vocabulary or the grammar. The teacher ignores the fundamentals of grammar, or the careful building of a basic vocabulary. The Orthodox method is designed to read the Hebrew text, and repeat what is learned, with its translation, by heart.

I can remember in Hebrew school the hours we'd spend sitting over our books. The teacher would read the verse and then give the translation, word for word. We'd repeat it after him. Then he'd move on to the next verse, and the next, and we'd repeat those too. Some words we learned along the way, so that we would recognize them. Some grammatical points we picked up, like male and female verb endings. But generally we only had to remember what it meant and say it back right.

After years of this kind of learning, you'll find men who can read Hebrew beautifully, and understand remarkably little.

They have minimal knowledge of the language. They can only recite the prayers they have learned by heart, intone the blessings they have memorized by rote, and translate in the old word-for-word style they have been taught.

This came home to me most clearly when I lived in Israel. Though I'd had years of Hebrew education, I could hardly speak a word. The Israeli government has set up an excellent system of intensive Hebrew courses, and within five months immigrants learn to speak, read and write Hebrew, even if they couldn't recognize the alphabet when they began. I took three months of one course, and learned more Hebrew then than in all the years of traditional teaching.

But the essence of the rabbinic approach is unequivocal. It doesn't matter if you understand it or not, as long as you repeat the prayers, read the blessings and observe the laws.

There's an extensive body of Hebrew poetry and literature, some of it from the 15th century when a thriving Jewish community lived in Spain, and some from more modern times. But Orthodox Jews ignore such literature. The language of Hebrew is reserved for prayer. They have little interest in learning a living tongue.

In most Orthodox study schools, the discussions take place in Yiddish, the accepted daily language for conversation.

The old traditions for teaching are designed to create clones to carry on the faith.

There are those who believe that the rabbinic students who spend days arguing over the points of religious law in the schools of rabbinic studies are somehow benefiting from an educational method worthy of serious consideration. It's a misplaced admiration.

I've sat and listened to these discussions, when they were held in English at seminars I attended. The system follows the same pattern as the laws which are being studied. These are lumped together in a totally haphazard fashion, together with interpretations, commentaries, stories, and legends. The meandering discussion on whether you can build a fence around your property or whether you may wear wool and linen together are debated with the same intense passion as a discussion on whether a man should be hanged for murder or whether a woman may divorce her husband if he is impotent. The object is a game of scoring points, making arguments, debating feverishly. But unlike a legal discussion in a law office, there are never any resolutions. At no point does someone say, "Well, now what shall we do about this?" The discussions are totally pointless, rooted in unreality, and unconnected to any decision or action.

In real life, passionate argument over an issue is usually followed by a decision. There's a responsibility attached to that decision. And the decision may be followed by action. That's how problems are solved, houses are built, emergencies are survived.

Years of aimless discussion in a religious training school can successfully teach most people to avoid coming to any conclusion. They can continue to bat the issues back and forth, bringing up obscure points of law or ancient sayings. They know how to divert attention from the issue at hand. And they have no understanding at all of logical thinking, of assembling facts, of assessing situations, of making deductions, of analyzing the possibilities, of weighing benefits against disadvantages, and of being able to make decisions and take action.

Their minds are successfully fogged up in an eternal wandering miasma. They eagerly leap to the next topic for discussion, be it childrearing or cheating or catastrophes. They are quite oblivious to the realities of the discussion; it's merely a pretext for animated examination, for pinpointing the details, for carrying the intellectual delights of what-if to the furtherest possibilities, and for ignoring the basic common sense of rational thought.

That's why the laws relating to Judaism are so nit-picking and detailed. The rabbis who made them up spent centuries debating each picayune point to its extreme conclusion of absurdity.

Women, who have normally been excluded from these experiences, generally approach religious issues with a more practical mindset. But they are intimidated by the onslaught of detailed rabbinic sayings which overrule any sensible thinking.

They are also taught to be impressed by the "learning" which is supposed to be going on in the rabbinic schools of study. And they are taught never to interrupt their husband if he's reading a religious book.

There's a sad Yiddish tale, about a woman with no money to buy food for her family, watching her children starve while her husband continues to study his religious texts. She interrupts her husband, to beg for money for food, but he says bitterly:

"Foolish woman, evil woman, not to allow your husband to study! For this you may burn in Hell!"

Even in Orthodox homes today, it's considered wrong to speak to a man who is studying or reading his text. An Orthodox woman who has studied family behavior within the Orthodox community notes that women hesitate to interrupt a man who is sitting reading a Hebrew text or supposedly studying "because they know that their question will be trivial compared to the importance of what he is studying."

Coping in the Modern Orthodox Style

My Jewish upbringing was intense, but fell somewhere between extreme Orthodox and modern. My parents were seriously devout, and observed many of the detailed rules for eating, observing the Sabbath and the holidays.

But they wore ordinary clothes. My father was a business-man, with an office in the city. His commitment to his reli-gion demanded that he come home early on Friday evenings, and not work on any of the holidays. We were all expected to observe the rules of the Sabbath from the lighting of the can-dles on Friday evening to the final ceremony of candle-lighting which marked the end of the Sabbath on Saturday evening, which is called Havdala. We were supposed to be able to spot three stars in the sky to make sure the Sabbath had ended.

My father went to all synagogue services, often going in the afternoon and the evening as well as the morning.

My mother acquiesced. She had no upbringing in Ortho-doxy, but she quickly absorbed what had to be done and what her husband expected. She knew the rules. She never learned to read Hebrew but stood through service after ser-vice turning the pages of her prayer book, unable to under-stand a word unless she read the English translation. She knew that appearance was everything. She preserved her ap-pearance of dutiful Orthodox wife. There was never any discussion. This was how it was, and she never questioned the ritual.

I wonder if my parents would choose an Orthodox school for me now. I do know that they certainly favored the idea of the local Jewish school. However, the daughters of several friends attended a prestigious girls' school with high aca-demic standards. I took the entrance examination and was accepted. Before they had quite decided that this was the right place for me, I won a scholarship to the age of eighteen.

Children accept what they are given, assuming that's the way it is everywhere. At school, I studied math and science and history, played sports and attended gym classes and learned how to use a potter's wheel.

Then I would come home to go to Hebrew classes on Sun-day mornings and for a couple of hours after school on Tuesdays and Thursdays. Here we'd study Hebrew texts, learn about the religious holidays, and absorb the messages of the Bible.

At school, I'd have biology classes where we talked about how tadpoles turned into frogs, how seeds were germinated and why climates differed.

At Hebrew classes, we'd learn about God creating the universe, and all within it, and how woman was created from man's rib.

At school, we'd study earthquakes, floods and the effects of drought. At Hebrew classes, we'd learn about the Red Sea dividing so that Moses and the children and Israel could escape from Pharaoh.

There were stern lectures in Hebrew school about not taking God's name in vain. When we studied a text, or practiced a prayer, and God's name appeared in the Hebrew, we had to learn to say "The Name" in Hebrew (Hashem) instead. Or if the word for "God" came up, which is "Elohim" we had to say "Elokim" which apparently changed it enough that it wasn't taken in vain. The word for "Jehovah" which is often written in the Bible and in prayers is never read as it is. Instead you have to say "Adonai" which is the Hebrew word for Lord.

It also applied in English. When we wrote about Jewish holidays or observances in English, we were not supposed to write down the name of God in full. I had notebooks full of "G–d", the acceptable form, from my days in Hebrew school. The logic of missing out the vowels still escapes me. It always seemed as if it would be more sensible to leave out the consonants and simply write "–o–". That way no one would be able to read the name, which I understood to be the reason for the subterfuge.

A few years ago, I was working as a temporary secretary in an office. A young woman on staff gave me some letters to retype with new addresses. There, in the middle of the letter was the phrase: "God knows when we'll hear about it." The word was carefully typed: "G–d."

At school, we studied ancient history, and the life of the people in Greek and Roman times. The Jews were a footnote, a group which existed but played a minor role in the great sweep of history.

At Hebrew classes, we learned only about the role of the Jews in Greek and Roman times. The other aspects of that world were dismissed completely.

At school, there was an acceptance of Christianity as the religion of the majority. It was impossible to avoid Christmas and the story of Jesus. Most of us knew the words of the carols everyone sang.

At Hebrew classes, we understood that no one ever mentioned the name of Jesus under any circumstances. You could talk about the terrible atrocities of the Spanish Inquisition of the 1500s when Jews suffered under Torquemada. You could certainly talk movingly about the terrible destruction of the Holocaust under Hitler in this century. And during the festival of Purim, the story of Haman, (who tried to persuade the king to kill all the Jews thousands of years ago in Persia), is read with appropriate noise-making whenever Haman's name is mentioned.

But any discussion of Jesus was taboo. It was an interesting denial. There was no Old and New testament. There was only the Bible, the Torah. We could not use B.C. for dates meaning Before Christ. Instead we were taught to say B.C.E., meaning, "Before the Common Era."

And A.D. meaning Anno Domini, the year of the Lord, was unacceptable. For those dates, we were supposed to write C.E. meaning the "Common Era."

We learned nothing about the spread of Christianity, or its development. We heard nothing of Christian suffering in defense of faith. We were kept in ignorance of the times when Christians and Jews and Moslems managed to live peaceably together.

I absorbed the idea that as soon as Jesus had arrived and started Christianity, Jews were persecuted for ever after.

It was only later when I read the New Testament and histories of the early years of Christianity that I understood how little we had been told about a crucial time in the history of the world.

I don't suppose Christian educators go out of their way to present the Jewish perspective. Nor do I suppose that Moslem teachers like to explain the Christian and the Jewish viewpoint.

But I think for Jews to completely ignore the advent of Christianity, to deny the impact it has had on the world, and to deprive children of an understanding of a major event in the development of the western culture is an unhealthy state of ignorance. It's as if they are frightened that even to teach about it may contaminate those who hear it.

The Schizophrenia of Orthodox Education

Many girls growing up today within the Orthodox community face the same dilemmas I experienced in my own education.

On one hand, there's encouragement to learn as much as possible, take advantage of every opportunity and step forward into the world of today where women have more freedom and more choices than ever before.

On the other hand, there's a persistent refrain that the only fulfillment acceptable to the Orthodox community is marriage, and motherhood.

Modern Orthodox Jews, who call themselves "centrist Orthodox," often send their children to Orthodox day schools, which have increased in number in recent years. There are now about fifty in the New York area. They meet state and national academic requirements, and provide an academic program equal to that of the public schools.

Many students continue their studies at university, often choosing a Jewish university where the Orthodox atmosphere is established.

Girls within these schools attend classes and study the same subjects as boys. They too are encouraged to continue their education. But at the same time, they live with the double message that they shouldn't be too bright; after all, they do have to get married.

Sandra, a television producer who runs her own company, remembers the feeling well. She attended an Orthodox school.

"My brothers went to the same school, and we were all encouraged to study hard, and do the best we could," she says. "But I know that my parents hoped that I'd marry and not go to college. They were really worried when I became interested in television and started working crazy hours at a local cable TV station in the summer. My father kept asking me why I had to be there all day for a half-hour program in the evening.

"One brother is now an accountant, and the other works in my father's clothing business. I think if I had wanted to do something acceptable, like teaching or medicine, they might have been more sympathetic. But they couldn't see why I went to work in Minneapolis for a television station. And they never wanted to hear about the independent shows I made about a senior citizens center or the news stories I covered.

"I knew that even getting married wouldn't help. I met a cameraman, who wasn't the least interested in an Orthodox Jewish wedding. He wanted us to write our own ceremony. And of course, we both planned to go on working in television."

She sighed. "No matter what they say, Orthodox parents want you to 'settle down.' There's no way they can understand the options out here in the real world. They just don't like the idea of independent women outside the community."

I can still remember when my teachers encouraged me to apply to university. My application form had to have a parental signature. My father refused to sign it, absolutely certain that it was wrong and detrimental for me to have any further education beyond the age of 18. There were great arguments. But it was only when my boyfriend at the time, whom I had met at a charity dance to which my parents had taken me, talked to my father, man to man, that he agreed to sign the application.

My mother, during this altercation, maintained her position of total agreement with my father. However, at the same time she urged me to take a secretarial course "so that I could get a job and support myself." The fact that a better education might lead to a better job was beyond her comprehension. Education was a waste of time; secretarial work was acceptable. It was a strangely confusing double message. Why would I need to support myself if I only had to get married?

5

The Bar Mitzva: The Great Divide Where Boys Become Men and Girls Realize They Have Failed

From the day he's born, parents of Jewish boys dream and prepare for their son's Bar Mitzva. It's like the anticipation and dreams of a wedding, but at least both sexes participate in that ceremony.

Jewish parents spend at least twelve years thinking about the event. Well, maybe they don't have it in the forefront of their minds all the time. But they let it slip into their thoughts as they see their son studying his Hebrew lessons. A fond look comes into their eyes when they see him walking to the synagogue with his father. And they smile gently as they watch other boys perform on their appointed Bar Mitzva day in the synagogue.

"One day, please God, he'll be Bar Mitzva," they whisper to themselves.

The preparations begin very early. The religious ceremony involves the boy being called to the scrolls of the Torah
during a Saturday morning service, and reading the portion
of the scroll. Since the first five books of the Bible, which
make up the Torah, are read chronologically, it's quite easy
to work out which section the boy will read. It's the one
closest to his thirteenth birthday, or often the Hebrew date
of his birthday, if his parents prefer to use the lunar Jewish
calendar.

Some fathers work out which portion will be assigned to
their son years ahead of time. It's a bit like putting a boy's
name down for a prestigious prep school at birth. And as the
years pass, the excitement mounts.

Generally around the twelfth birthday, the first steps are
taken to formalize the upcoming occasion. The father speaks
to the rabbi, or whoever is in charge of the calendar for the
community, and the date is set.

It is as demanding, as involving and as emotionally
charged a time as any preparation for a major landmark in
life. For the next year, everything will revolve around the
Bar Mitzva and the boy for whom these events are planned.

First, he has to have lessons in order to learn the portion
which he is going to read. Then he will also have to learn to
read the symbols which indicate the chanting and tune of the
sing-song recitation traditionally used. He will also decide if
he is going to read only a portion, or if he wants to read the
weekly portion from the prophets as well.

At the same time, there's the big family party side of the
celebration. To be honest about it, most young boys understand this aspect of the event far better than the religious
side. And certainly their sisters recognize very quickly that
the boys enjoy parties, presents and undiluted attention at
the Bar Mitzva in a way that no girl ever does. There's no way
to hide the gifts, the money and the aura of glory which sur-
rounds a young boy at thirteen as he experiences his Bar
Mitzva. It's visible to the entire community.

For the months before the Bar Mitzva and on the day itself, he will be the center of attention in his own circle. I can
still remember from my days at Hebrew school how the

teacher would find out which boys were going to be Bar Mitzva, and ask them about their portion, what they were reading, who they were studying with, how they were getting along. It was a man-to-man discussion, ignoring the girls in the room, who would have no part of this experience.

The build-up toward "The Day" is rather like the countdown to the launch of a space rocket. Everything has to focus on the one event, to the exclusion of all other concerns.

And since Orthodox Jews are human beings, just like everyone else, there's an enormous amount of pressure, tension and downright conflict going on for a great deal of the time.

Jack Rosenthal wrote a wonderful television play called "The Bar Mitzva Boy" which satirizes the family situation before the event. Here's the mother trying to plan the dinner after the service, and wondering what to wear, and when to get her hair done. There's the father trying to keep the atmosphere calm while coping with phone calls from relatives arriving from around the world. And the over-burdened boy, a sensitive twelve-year-old, suddenly decides he cannot go through with the event, and runs away. It's a beautiful portrayal of a very familiar scenario.

Jewish folklore, like the folklore of many other religious groups, perpetuates the myth that its family life is stronger, healthier and holier than anyone else's. There have been no studies of the trauma and crises of the pre-Bar Mitzva period in an Orthodox Jewish household. It's a time of tensions. Parents argue over who is coming. Wives shout angrily at husbands about who sits with whom at the dinner. Brothers and sisters watch warily as the pressures build.

The youngster himself spends months in a state of anguished apprehension, terrified he will embarrass his family in front of the community and dreading his moment of performance when he will be called to the Reading of the Law.

It's also a kind of bonding with the male members of the community, who have experienced the same agonies. Or perhaps there were less pressures in smaller communities, and they embraced the event with an assurance and ability they expect to see in every boy.

My brother confounded the preparations by catching chicken pox the week before the event. So everything had to be postponed, with telegrams going out to relatives and friends, and the minister rescheduling the reading.

Other young boys almost faint as they read. Or stand there petrified hardly able to speak. Or stutter their way through the reading. But they have no choice. If the law says they must be Bar Mitzva, they must be Bar Mitzva.

Why Girls Are Ignored

I realized quite early in my childhood that I would never have a Bar Mitzva, or its feminine equivalent, a Bat Mitzva. Orthodox teaching is unequivocal.

I don't remember exactly when I knew. I'm sure I asked my parents why. "That's the law," they would have replied. Perhaps I asked my teachers. They too would have brushed me off with didactic statements like, "Girls don't have them," or perhaps looked forward to the day of my wedding, the one major Jewish event when a woman participates in a service.

But I have thought about it over the years. I know it rankled when I did well in Hebrew school, and learned to read the prayers fluently, and even picked up the sing-song traditional recitation, since I could sing well.

I was a member of a children's group where we learned modern Hebrew and Israeli dances, and stories about the development of present-day Israel.

But in all these activities, I realized that my role was to be perpetually subsidiary to the boys in the group. The boys sat with their fathers in the synagogue, actively involved in the service, watching the Torah scrolls being taken around, and clearly in charge.

Once, one of the more outspoken women in the community publicly suggested that the women should be able to vote in synagogue elections and run for office just like the men. She was ridiculed and laughed at. But I can remember the sudden shock of realization that her suggestion gave me. I knew that she was absolutely right.

It's hard for parents to pretend it doesn't matter if they only have daughters, or if their eldest child is a daughter, because it clearly makes an enormous difference.

Having a son who has a Bar Mitzva is an essential part of Jewish life, reflecting centuries of traditional observance. It's a major celebration, remembered throughout one's lifetime, to be recounted and repeated at family occasions again and again. The little things that happen, the odd comments, the jokes, the moments of excitement are high points of an experience which is the central focus of family life for months on end.

Often, parents will have a large photograph of their son in his first prayer shawl at his Bar Mitzva placed in a prominent place in the house. At home we had a photo of my parents with my brother at his Bar Mitzva which was one of their favorites.

It's not something that can be dismissed lightly, or ignored. The attention given to a boy's Bar Mitzva is an enormous upheaval in a family's experience, and something that no girl can help but notice. I was older than my brother, who was extremely nervous about the pressure of his Bar Mitzva. I sympathized with his months of tension, when he threw up and grew even more nervous as the day drew near. But at the same time, I was well aware that my thirteenth birthday was not different from my twelfth or my fourteenth. I had simply had a party for my friends, with the usual cake and presents. There had been absolutely no religious or social significance to that celebration.

The Code of Jewish Law does not even consider the idea of a ceremony for girls at the age of thirteen. According to the *Woman's Guide to Jewish Observance*, by Rabbi Yitzhak Yaacov Fuchs, designed for Orthodox and Hasidic families, the idea is a myth.

"A Bat Mitzva celebration is not a 'mitzvah' [commandment or good deed]" he intones, "and it should not be held in a synagogue."

A girl is considered an adult when she has reached the age of twelve—a year before boys. After that she is supposed to observe all the "mitzvot" (commandments) that adult Jewish women may keep. According to one Talmudic interpretation, she's reached physical maturity when she has at least two pubic hairs.

There is no mention that I can find of defining a boy's maturity by his pubic hairs. Perhaps there are secret pubic hair counting ceremonies which I've been excluded from. But there are no detailed discussions about the physical development of boys and how to judge them. What's more, I wonder who counts the girl's pubic hairs? Surely they wouldn't dare leave that to mothers, who are helpless women? Perhaps the all-purpose-black-bearded rabbi is called in once again.

However, it's permissible to hold a party or private celebration for a girl, as long as the celebration "conforms to the standards of modest behavior."

It's like giving one child a diamond, highly valued in the community, and the other a cheap piece of glass, pretending she won't notice the difference. After all, no one has ever complained before!

But who is there to complain to? You certainly can't tell the rabbi that you think it's unfair for boys to have an official Bar Mitzva and girls to be ignored.

You can't go to the women of the community. They have been through it all, and they are too browbeaten to think of protest. Enough already! You'll have a party, a few friends, and that's the way it is!

You can't go to historical example. Had any woman or girl ever protested or criticized the situation, no record would have been kept of the rebellion. What rabbi would record the success of opposition to a male-dominated society? Why register that an entire community objected to the fact that girls were ignored, should that have happened?

This lop-sided recording of Jewish life first came to my attention when I was researching the role of interfaith marriages in Jewish life. It was desperately difficult to find any record of such occurrences, and yet Moses himself, in the Bible, had married a non-Jewish woman. Surely there were other such events throughout history? But no scribe or rabbi or recordkeeper noted them, because it was offensive to those who kept the books.

"We All Want to Keep It the Traditional Way"

Traditionalists deny that there's criticism, opposition or downright rebellion against the status quo. The image to perpetuate is one of dedicated harmony within a united community. Transgressors are always misguided, unfortunate and doomed to misery. A united front is essential to suppress dissenters.

As soon as he can hear, a little boy is lured forward with the magical promise of his Bar Mitzva. And behind him, the little girl, no matter how eager, how dedicated a student or how observant in her practices, will realize that her achievements are unimportant.

This isn't exactly explained as succinctly as I've put it. There's a kind of parental hypocrisy which Orthodox Jewish parents are forced to adopt, which once again disrupts any possible unity within the family. They see the jealousy that erupts because of the favoritism toward their sons, so they assert that both children are equal in their sight.

In their own hearts, this may well be true. There is love for every child in a parent's caring and feeding. But in a society where boys are valued above girls, it's crystal clear that the love outside the family, in the community where a parent's status is judged by sons, is biased against their daughters.

It is sad to admit that this is so. But the truth is visibly evident. In the synagogue services, all the boys sit by their fathers and are encouraged to sing, chant and take an active part in the service. The girls are sent to sit with their mothers, behind a screen, behind a curtain, upstairs, secreted away, not worthy of participation and enjoined not to sing or chant lest their voices be heard.

During the prayers which a Jewish man recites every morning are a series of blessings, which include: "Thank you, Lord, for not making me a non-Jew, for not making me a slave, for not making me a woman."

When women say the prayers, an alternate version is suggested. But no Orthodox authority has yet ordered any change in the men's prayers.

I once had a long discussion with a Jewish writer who believed deeply that he was glad that he had not been made a woman, and felt the prayer was very important. I tried to point out that it was demeaning and insulting for me to be lumped together with non-Jews and slaves, and that the tone of the prayer was not complimentary to women. He said that women had to bear children, and suffer pain, and take an inferior role in the world, so he was glad not to be one. I said that times were changing.

"Why don't women say that they are glad not to be created a man?" I suggested.

"That's outrageous!" he exclaimed angrily. "Why would anyone not be glad to be created a man?"

"I am!" I said, looking at the astonishment on his face. "I think women have a great many experiences and advantages that men will never know, and I feel men are deprived of many things that women enjoy."

He looked at me in disbelief. "That's ridiculous!"

Now this conversation with an intelligent, educated man reflected a view that is commonly held by Orthodox men. To try to persuade a rabbi or religious leader that the time has come to revise the insult of that particular prayer would be extraordinarily difficult.

Every day throughout his life my father and his friends, and later my brother and his friends, and Jews in every Orthodox synagogue and home in every part of the world, have repeated that ancient prayer, reinforcing the notion that somehow it is bad to be a woman, and men must thank God daily for not inflicting that terrible misfortune upon them.

It's not an annual ceremonial prayer. It's not a special recitation reflecting perhaps a unique point of view in Jewish observance. This prayer is an integral part of the Orthodox perspective, ingrained into the fundamental concepts of faith. And it's repeated every single day by every single Orthodox man over the age of thirteen.

Family Quarrels

This one-sided view of the human race has a disastrous effect on family harmony. It's difficult for any family of adults and children to work out a way of living together compatibly. In a family where the boys are singled out for extra attention and the girls ignored, the tensions are exacerbated from day one.

Boys automatically assume that this is the way the world is, and accept the warped and unrealistic interpretations of female behavior given by the rabbis. They respond to the jealousy with the security of their position. They know they are the masters of the faith and that women are subservient.

"I couldn't wait to get out of the house," said one young woman. "The constant harping on my older brother's career and his school and his Bar Mitzva was insane. Nothing I did ever mattered—and it took me years to realize what was happening."

In the ceremonies at home, it is the father who chants the blessings and takes action. The mother lights candles on Friday evening and festivals. But she isn't the one who says the blessing over the wine, or the fresh bread, which she may have baked. Nor does she lead the grace after meals. Nor is she allowed to carry out the candle-lighting ceremony, Havdala, at the end of the Sabbath. She is limited to lighting two candles.

And she has no need to perform the daily prayers which the Orthodox Jewish male recites each day, binding the strange black boxes on his head and his arm with long black straps. Instead, she can be busy getting him his breakfast and cleaning the house and caring for the children.

The children watch all of this. The sons know that they will soon take on the honors of prayer; the daughters learn they will soon become the slaves of the household. There are no alternatives. And there's no arena for complaints. There is no concept of equality; it's a master-and-slave role. Individual variations and personal characteristics may sway the balance; but in the final struggle, the woman is helpless, tied to the man in a community run by men with rules devised by men.

It's interesting that recent studies of child development show that by depriving girls of participation in a ceremony marking the years of puberty, they are being mistreated at a particularly sensitive time of their mental and emotional growth.

Matina Horner's studies of success in women show that it is precisely at this stage, between seventh and eighth grades when children are twelve and thirteen, that girls begin to question the relationship between their femininity and their ability to succeed.

"In the rite of Bat Mitzva, the girl is shown that her femininity is being affirmed, by her successful completion of a difficult intellectual task," says Cherie Koller-Fox, a doctoral candidate in education at Harvard University, writing in *The Jewish Woman: New Perspectives.*

"Girls at this age need a number of crucial things which the Bat Mitzva offers them in a Jewish context—a chance for large-scale communal validation, and a chance to have an extended period of personal attention and validation from an adult as part of the preparation for the event," she states.

Orthodox Judaism dismisses observations like these without a second thought. If the rabbis didn't want to give girls the same ceremony as boys, they say firmly, then nothing is ever going to change that fact.

A Reform Option

Let's take a look at the benefits change might bring. Indeed, for the world of the future where women will play a role as yet undefined by the beliefs and patterns of the past, the situation within Orthodoxy and Hasidim cries out for change.

A friend invited me to the ceremony of her daughter's Bat Mitzva in a Reform temple. From the moment I arrived, the feeling was completely different. Men and women sat together, husbands with wives, mothers with sons. On the "bima," the platform, there was a rabbi and a cantor. The rabbi happened to be a man; the cantor happened to be a woman. The service included the Reading from the Torah. Both the mother and father were called to join their daughter in her recitation. Both participated in the blessings and the traditional recitations, just as both had participated in bringing her up from birth.

The daughter read her portion fluently and with confidence. She was assured and yet tinged with the nervousness of a child at a great event. Watching her carry out her duties with the conviction of a person who believed in her faith and was valued in herself, I realized how different Orthodox Judaism could be if girls were seen as human beings, not embryo sexual temptresses.

The ceremony was moving. The congregation listened devoutly. There was a warm quiet of concentration and involvement. And afterwards, there was a lunch and party in the adjoining hall, where men and women together celebrated the happy moment of a Jewish child reaching the age of adulthood.

Sometimes I describe this experience to Orthodox men and women. They listen politely, their faces blank. When I suggest that it's a great idea, they shake their heads.

"It's impossible" said one man firmly. "You can't call women to read from the Torah."

"But why not?"

"It's impossible," he said, angrily.

Nothing is impossible. But within Orthodoxy, a pattern of thinking has been set for so many years that it's hard to envisage a different arrangement.

The Talmud at one point says, "All are qualified to be among the seven [who read from the Torah scrolls during synagogue services] even a minor and a woman."

Women are included after children, but at least they are included.

However, within Orthodoxy over the years an impenetrable thicket of teachings and sayings and ruling have been repeated and reinforced to persuade everyone that women cannot be called to read from the Torah scrolls. There are strict regulations about a woman's behavior during the time she is menstruating, which I will discuss later in detail. She is not allowed to go near the Torah during that time, because she is "unclean." However, there are plenty of older women who no longer menstruate, and presumably those laws would hardly apply to them.

Reason and rational argument are not the issue; the men don't want women interfering in their sacred preserves.

This attitude is clearly demonstrated in the male response to a group of devout Orthodox Jewish women who decided they wanted to pray together. They were not radicals, advocating change. They wanted more from their faith.

In 1982, five Orthodox Jewish women in Brooklyn formed a women-only prayer group because they objected to the separation and isolation in the synagogue. They wanted to participate in prayer with true fervor and devotion.

The response to this simple step shocked them. *The Jewish Press,* a New York paper, called them "a very right wing group" and issued a ban on women-only prayer groups, printed in a box with a thick black band.

Then rabbis spoke out against them from the pulpit, criticizing the group and forbidding other women to follow their example. Five rabbis at Yeshiva University issued a statement denouncing them. The University is under the auspices of the Rabbinical Council of America, the center of Orthodox Judaism.

Rivka Haut, one of the founding members, told a writer of *New Directions for Women,* a feminist newsletter:

"That really hurt. . . . They said our motives were impure; that we were not doing this for religious reasons but out of rebellion and for our own glorification. They asked, why can't we be normal women? They didn't talk to us. The charges were based on hearsay and misconceptions."

She points out that the group is doing nothing wrong.

"We pray, we hold baby-namings, engagements, Bat Mitzvas. We're very family-oriented . . . To a great extent, we're bunch of married, middle-aged religious women."

Today the group rents space in a Conservative synagogue for its services, because all the Orthodox congregations they approached refused them. By 1985, there were women's prayer groups in several other cities, and about 250 members belong to the Women's "Tefillah" (Prayer) Network. They have bi-monthly meetings, publish a quarterly newsletter and have held a conference. The major focus of the Network is the education of girls.

It's a disturbing insight into a closed community which discriminates against girls at birth and at puberty. When faced with a group which quietly wants to ease some of the emotional pain endured over the centuries in synagogues, the men immediately try to suppress their small step for independence.

No Women Wanted Here

Women find it hard to believe that men don't like them. Men simply don't want them around, interfering in the centuries-old traditions of Jewish prayer. They don't want them commenting on the male-only world of rabbinic interpretations. It's a club they don't want women to join.

There are no halfway measures in Orthodoxy. I'm always surprised by the earnest compromises suggested by some Jewish feminists trying to reach out and find a middle ground which includes women in the observances of Orthodoxy. There isn't any. The only solution is a radical rewriting of the interpretation of the Torah, the five books of Moses with its subsequent laws and customs, to eliminate all vestiges of sexism. And to appoint a committee of women rabbis to do the rewriting.

Men in Orthodox Judaism, particularly its more extremist branches, want to keep things just the way they are today. No man really wants to see his daughter breaking with tradition and having a fully fledged Bat Mitzva where she will read from the Torah: it offends his sense of propriety. No man really wants to have his wife actively involved in services, when he can enjoy the benefits of honors and prayer without her.

Fathers may placate daughters who criticize the discrimination of ceremonies for boys but not for girls. But in their hearts, they know they really don't want things to be different.

The whole concept of a boy becoming a man at the age of thirteen is, of course, a delusion. It's a symbolic gesture to recognize the passage from child to adult, but it certainly doesn't happen overnight between the ages of twelve and thirteen.

Thirteen-year-old boys are still boys, and often are less mature than thirteen-year-old girls. There is no significant change at the age of thirteen. Puberty commences at different times for different children, and in the teenage years many changes take place until a child is fully grown.

By singling out boys and ignoring girls at this significant point in life, Orthodox Judaism demeans women and damages their self-esteem. This is not the same as the circumcision or Redemption of the Firstborn ceremonies. Both of these take place within the family, and the baby is unlikely to remember what happened clearly.

But to emphasize the experience of a Bar Mitzva for a boy and to deny that experience to a girl is to draw a line of sharp distinction which does not in reality exist.

Boys and girls develop, grow, think, experiment and experience joy and pain in much the same proportions. If they both prepare for an event to mark the onset of puberty, if they both learn the demands and the challenges of the experience, and if they both feel a sense of achievement and success at what they can do, they will have a better understanding of their own abilities and of each other.

The Bar Mitzva is a public ceremony, held in the synagogue in full view of all the congregation, parents and relatives, friends and acquaintances. It is announced in publications, mentioned as an event of note, and is part of the ancient traditions of Judaism.

The message a girl receives is that she is unable to fulfill this duty, she is not permitted to show that she can read from the Torah, and she is considered unworthy of appearing before the congregation.

In the years when I was growing up, I watched many young boys read their portion from the Torah, listen to the official sermon urging them to grow up to be devout and honorable young men, and then receive the gift from the minister of a Bible. They were always urged to "Read what is in it and you will be well read; keep what is in it and you will be well kept."

Before my own thirteenth birthday, I watched with a certain fascination, wondering what it felt like. But afterwards, I slowly realized that the ceremony was a slap in the face to all the years I had studied so hard in Hebrew school, to all the dedication I had felt to my faith, and to all the effort I had expended to be a good Jewish girl.

No one was the least interested in my ability to read and understand Hebrew, or my knowledge of Judaism. My role as a girl was unimportant. I could be as ignorant as the stupidest student in the class. If I were a boy, I'd be able to have a Bar Mitzvah, and be recognized as a worthy member of the congregation. But as a girl, I and my girlfriends were ignored. Our role was to sit upstairs, separate, almost invisible, and let the men show us what to do.

It was the beginning of my disillusionment.

6

Adolescence: The Essence of Repression and When I Began to Think of Escape

It's pimples and acne. It's pain and parental confusion. It's paranoia that no one in the whole world understands. It's puberty, "the development of secondary sexual characteristics," as the textbooks so calmly describe it, which turns boys and girls into men and women.

Modern studies of human development, childhood and adolescence have discovered a great deal about this time of change. Research shows that it's stressful, significant, and as much a challenge to parents as to the growing teenager.

Orthodox Judaism and Hasidic authorities don't even mention it.

I've looked it up in the index of several reference tomes. But there's no "adolescence" among Orthodox Jewish teenagers, according to the law.

I've studied several texts to see if there's any rabbinic advice on this stage of development. So far, I haven't discovered a thing.

Boys and girls are children, subject to the rules about obeying their parents and taking responsibility for some of their actions. Then, suddenly, they are adults. After their Bar Mitzva, boys are considered as men in synagogue services, and are urged to marry early.

The one quotation which seems to recognize the onset of adolescence is clear in its message:

"The Sages have ordained that a man should give his sons and daughters in marriage immediately upon their reaching maturity, for if he neglects them, they are apt to commit adultery, or entertain prurient thoughts."

That pretty well summarizes the Hasidic and ultra-Orthodox attitudes. The options are few. You marry, you commit adultery, or think naughty thoughts.

There are no other alternatives. There's no thought that a young woman might like to study to be a doctor, and delay her marriage. Or that a young man might like to travel independently, and decide on his future career before marrying. Or that the experience of meeting other men and women in adolescence might provide an education in human behavior which would help a marriage decision.

Once you decide to live by the Bible, it's tough to adjust to the present day, and the change of behavior and opportunities. So the rabbis choose to enforce their backwards attitudes and ignore adolescence.

Contrasting the Options

To illustrate how life can differ for teenage girls in the twentieth century as they look ahead to the twenty-first, let's compare the lives of two young women.

Debby is the eldest daughter. She goes daily to an all-girls Hasidic school, learning Hebrew and Judaic studies most of the day, with some math and language skills.

Alisa is the child of a Reform Jewish family, attending a public school with boys and girls, where there are high academic standards and a strong program in science and math, as well as foreign languages and literature.

Let's look at Alisa's day first. She studies chemistry, Spanish, French and Latin. She plays on the girls' soccer team, swims for her school and is a back-up player on the tennis team. She is a member of the school drama club, has a small part in the school play, is learning the piano and sings in the school choir.

Last summer, she went on an exchange visit to live with a family in Mexico. The summer before she hiked through state parks with a group, camping out, learning to canoe and cooking over a campfire. She's also helped at a day camp for handicapped children.

Her friends come from different backgrounds. She's met Suki, a Japanese girl, and she has begun to understand the difficulties of adjusting to a new culture and a new society.

At home, she finds it hard to balance homework, school demands and her responsibility for occasional evenings looking after her two younger sisters.

But her father encourages her to see that task as part of her contribution to family organization. There's a great deal of time on weekends spent preparing meals together, and talking. Both her parents appreciate and praise her struggles to keep up with work at school, and her sports activities.

From childhood, there's been an openness about sexual matters. Alisa know that she can turn to her mother with things that bother her. She has eagerly prepared for her first period, since she wants to be "grown-up" like one of her friends at school. She's also talked to her younger sisters, and answered their questions. She's a lively, warm, outgoing young girl, slowly developing into a confident young woman.

Over in the Hasidic community, it's hard for Debby to develop into an educated, competent young woman.

No one asks her to try. From the start, she's been made to feel inferior because she's a girl. Since there are no boys in the family, she knows that her mother has failed too. There's been no Bar Mitzva celebrations, and their father has little interest in what the girls are doing.

"Please God they'll marry soon and well!" he says on occasion. There are general nods of agreement from friends and relatives that that would indeed be an ideal solution to the problem of three daughters.

She goes to religious school, where she meets other girls like herself. The curriculum is limited; half the day is spent on reading, writing, and mathematics, and the other half on religious studies.

There is no science teaching, no biology, no human development classes, no sports for the girls. They play outside on the paved yard by the building. There are no teams to join, no tennis games to watch, no drama club for her, no choir for boys and girls to sing together.

It's made clear to her that she can learn to be a teacher in a religious school, or work with children, or stay at home and help her mother. Her schooling will end her education, and after that she knows that her parents are hoping that she will marry soon.

She has learned to be ashamed of her body, hidden as it is under the regulation layers of long stockings and high collars and long sleeves. She learns to keep her emotional and physical changes to herself as she grows up. She has no idea what caused the changes, and simply copes with them in embarrassed secrecy.

She has never travelled very far. Once she visited relatives in another part of the country, who were also Orthodox Jews. Once she went with her parents to a seashore hotel, for a week's vacation with a group from the synagogue. But she has never travelled anywhere on her own or stayed with another family, or visited anyone from another way of life. She is in awe of men, and suspicious of all non-Jews.

If you take a look through Biblical literature or even Talmudic commentaries, you'll find it hard to spot a young girl anywhere. Certainly the Great Women, like Sarah, the wife of Abraham, or Rachel, the wife of Jacob, or Leah, Rachel's sister, have no youth. They appear as grown women and are married off.

The only suggestion of a young independent girl comes in the story of Moses. If you remember, the Pharaoh issued an edict that all Jewish baby boys must be killed. However, Moses' mother determined to save her child. She made a cradle to float down the river to safety. By chance, it was discovered by the Pharaoh's daughter, when she and her handmaidens were bathing in the river. She was delighted with the baby.

It was Miriam, Moses' sister, who watched over the floating cradle. She was the one who saw the handmaidens of Pharaoh's daughter bring the baby to her. And she was the one who boldly came forward and offered to find a nurse for the child, and then brought her mother to apply for the position.

That's one of the few instances of a young girl behaving in a responsible and positive manner, without getting married, or having a baby.

What's more, no one commented on the fact that Pharaoh's unmarried daughter adopted Moses and brought him up, acting as a single parent. The man to whom God entrusted the Ten Commandments was brought up by Egyptians, never went to a religious school, and later married a Midianite woman, a non-Jew.

Naughty Things About Bodies Are Ignored

Despite the ostrich attitudes of the authorities, young people still experience puberty. What kind of information do Orthodox and Hasidic parents give to their daughters about the changes in their bodies and the experience of physical development?

Very little, and it emphasizes the negative aspects.

We're back in the mid-Victorian era, when bare legs on pianos were covered with frilly pantaloons so as not to embarrass people. Discussions of bodies and physical change are Not Nice. The Orthodox simply like to emphasize the importance of prayer and devotion and observance, and ignore the compelling concerns of the twelve-year-old girl who suddenly realizes her chest is growing bumpier. Whatever explanation she is given by her mother, a friend, or an older sister, it will be a message of embarrassment and subterfuge. From the very first, it's made clear within extremist families that physical development is not to be discussed openly, and that girls particularly must keep their experiences hidden.

As in many religious communities, children pick up bits

and pieces of information about their bodies, and muddle through in ignorance of what is happening.

I grew up in an era when the word "menstruation" was not printed casually in magazines and newspapers. It was not a topic for family discussion. And my mother, bound within the repressive rules of her own upbringing and her present Orthodox life, was not in the least interested in talking to me about such an embarrassing topic. In this she was like many mothers of that generation.

I can remember telling her that I had learned about "periods" from friends in school. With the studied indifference of one who does not want to hear about it, she ignored me. The message was clear; do not bring up this topic with me.

When I first began bleeding one day in school, I was too embarrassed and ashamed to tell anyone. Finally, hours after I had come home, I told my mother, "I'm bleeding."

She understood, but said nothing. She sent me to my bedroom, and brought in a box of napkins, a belt and a booklet, the kind you get inside the box. Then she left.

The booklet was the first sensible explanation of what was going on. However, working out what you did with the napkins and the belt was more difficult. I had little idea where I was bleeding from, and it took me a while to understand the napkin went between the legs hooked on to the belt.

My mother did not refer to the matter again. It was made clear that she did not want to talk about it further. We could discuss what I would wear to the synagogue the next day, and what happened at school, and whose birthday party I was going to next week—but nothing else.

Within today's extreme Orthodox and Hasidic communities, the changes of the outside world toward women's health and sexuality are ignored. A young girl does not have access to the magazines and publications of today which assure her about her body and encourage her to feel confident about her development. Instead she learns the ancient fears and superstitions about bleeding and about being unclean.

It was at school where I learned for the first time about human reproduction and sexuality in my informative biology

class. Religious schools eliminate the subject. Young girls
caught behind the walls of religious extremism are deprived
of basic health information about human life, and are never
given educational facts to prepare them for the sexuality of
adulthood.

The boys are equally deprived of information. They also
glean what they can from gossip among friends, with the
usual secrecy and embarrassment of adolescence.

For them too, the world faces into the past, depriving them
of any understanding of change in relationships between
men and women.

One mother, whose three sons have grown up in the family's Reconstructionist Jewish faith, is very relieved that the
boys have seen her participation in services and observances.

"They know I do more than just light candles or serve
meals," she said. "They've seen women actively involved in
all aspects of faith, and men helping at home. That's very important for their own future lives."

Education has always been revered within Judaism. A man
who studies is respected in the community. Praise is always
lavished on the rabbis who spent years in religious academies
studying throughout their lives.

But the emphasis has been on study of the Torah and its
interpretations. Today, there are seminars and study groups
at many synagogues to encourage members to continue
learning more about Judaism, like Bible classes in churches.

In the past as today, there are only a handful of similar
groups organized for women. It's tradition for women to be
deprived of knowledge about the Torah, and to learn to defer to husbands and rabbis for religious decisions.

At the same time, Judaism takes great pride in the accom-
plishments of those who leave the world of Orthodoxy and
achieve academic distinction in the world outside, as doctors,
professors, scientists, or mathematicians. Once again, the
praise is directed to the men who have made their mark in
the world of secular learning.

Women are not part of these achievements. There is no
Jewish history to tell the Orthodox and Hasidic leaders how
to cope with the new wave of educated Jewish women. They

have no precedent for dealing with a young woman who decides she wants to go to medical school and become a doctor, like the famous Maimonides of the past. They don't know how to deal with a woman who says she prefers to concentrate on her professional career as a biologist instead of devoting herself to housework. And they can't even face the issue of a woman professor who decides she will remain single and live alone.

"A single Jewish woman is often a nonperson, whether she is single by choice or by circumstances, and whether she is never married, widowed or divorced," notes Susan Weidman Schneider, editor of *Jewish and Female; Choices and Changes in Our Lives Today*. "This disapproval is hardly restricted to dusty tomes. One prominent East Coast male rabbi, commenting on the large number of single Jews in New York City (estimated conservatively as 125,000), says: 'It's disgusting.'"

During adolescence, young girls are single. The thoughts of the future and what they can do with their lives reflect their education, their abilities and their family environment. But the message is overwhelmingly clear: "Marry!"

Rabbi R. M. Yellin, writing in *Conservative Judaism* magazine says that "anyone who feels that getting married or having children is oppressive or gets in the way of realizing identity reflects a posture that cannot exist normatively within the Jewish system."

The rigid Bible-based interpretation of a woman's role eliminates the myriad of options offered to women today. The rabbis have taken a quick glance through the window, and pulled the blinds down . . . to keep women sitting in the dark. The message to teenage girls is the way it was in the past.

Waking Up

My strongest memory of the years of my adolescence is a sense of waking up. It's as if I was ensconced in a comforting fog of dreams, and suddenly, I was shaken awake.

The years following my *not* having any kind of Bat Mitzva

at thirteen were a time of much soul-searching. I still went to Hebrew school, but I noticed that almost all the girls dropped out. We studied Hebrew grammar, and more advanced texts. But it was made clear that while I could continue to learn more, there was no role for me. Learning is highly revered within Judaism, so that I was "Doing Good" by studying more. But I was hampered by being female, which was "Not Good."

I began to wonder why on earth I bothered to learn more when there was nothing I could do with these studies. I began to attend fewer and fewer classes, and finally, I stopped going.

Then I became sharply aware of the discrimination of synagogue services.

I don't know why this loomed so strongly, when I'd been going along dutifully with my mother for some years. But at about fourteen or fifteen, I felt outraged that I had to go to synagogue, sit through lengthy services and always sit isolated upstairs, never to be accepted as part of the service. I also discovered strong objections to many of the prayers.

Take the opening blessing of part of the synagogue service for example:

"Blessed be He who spoke, and the world came into being; Blessed be He. Blessed be He [sic] who created the universe. Blessed be He who says and performs. Blessed be He who decrees and fulfills. Blessed be He who has mercy on the world. Blessed be He who has mercy on all creatures. Blessed be He who grants a goodly reward to those who revere him.

"Blessed be He who lives forever and exists eternally. Blessed be He who redeems and saves; blessed be His Name. Blessed art Thou, Lord our God, King of the Universe, O God, merciful Father, who are praised by the mouth of thy people, lauded and glorified by the tongue of Thy faithful servants.

"With the songs of Thy servant David will we praise Thee, Lord our God; with his hymns and psalms will we exalt, extol and glorify Thee. We will call upon Thy Name and proclaim Thee King, our King, Our God, Thou who are One, the life of the universe, O King, praised and glorified be Thy great name, forever and ever. Blessed art Thou, O Lord, King extolled with hymns of praise."

The obsequiousness of the approach appalled me. And I felt it especially offensive to sneak in the "Blessed be He who grants a goodly reward to those who revere him," as if the Lord might forget that point. It all sounded extraordinarily naive when I began to read it carefully.

How about a more sympathetic, modest and quiet God, who appreciated the simpler less adulatory aspects of prayer? I began to feel that my father's daily repetition of "Thank you Lord for not making me a woman," which he said each morning, was a statement I could not go on ignoring.

Orthodox synagogue services are not peaceful. I'm always amused by those who want to bring prayer into the public schools and who suggest a time of quiet prayer as a way of covering all faiths.

Orthodox Judaism does not have quiet prayers. They're sung and chanted and gabbled through and repeated and spoken and said and murmured and shouted in a variety of ways. They're often accompanied, particularly among Hasidim, by a frenzied shaking and bowing of the body to denote fervor.

During services there's always a hum of voices and, in many cases, much more. Gossip, discussion, conversations go on through the long-drawn-out Orthodox and Hasidic services, and sometimes the leader will bang on the floor or speak out to request silence.

In my over-sensitive adolescent view, the way services took place and the words of the prayers were not to my liking. I didn't want to prostrate myself before the Lord, and obey His every word. I wanted to rewrite the prayers. And I wanted a more respectful atmosphere.

So I stopped going to synagogue.

My parents, like many well-meaning religious parents whose children suddenly rebel, tried several persuasive methods to win me back.

First my mother told me she liked me to come with her. As

in many Orthodox families, the father and sons go early to the beginning of the services. The wives and daughters, who are mere appendages to the proceedings, go later.

"It's nice to have someone to walk with," she would say. I'd succumb and go with her.

But then I decided that was foolish. At some point I'd have to stop, and she'd have to go alone.

Then she told me it would upset my father. I'm not sure if she used the much-repeated "break-your-father's-heart" line then, or later. I knew how much he loved the image of The Perfect Family, the four of us walking home together, his role as Father clearly visible and the three of us demurely following his lead.

But then I realized that, too, was only a temporary argument. If I was going to stop going, my father would have to realize it too.

The issues of why I didn't want to go were unimportant to my family. When I tried to explain my concerns, they were brushed aside.

"You are supposed to go and that's what you have to do," said my mother firmly. "After all, what will other people think if you don't go?"

"But I don't believe in the prayers, and I don't like the way the service is conducted," I protested with the adolescent dream of perfection.

"Believe indeed!" sniffed my mother. "Nobody's going to ask you what you believe. Who knows what anybody believes? You're just supposed to go to the services—that's what you have to do."

It was a moment of awakening. The idea that most of the people who came to the synagogue were coming because they knew they had to come, or felt they ought to come, or had been told to come, and not from any spiritual motive, was a revelation. But, I wondered, in my newly found mood of questioning, why did they bother if they didn't believe it?

"It's good thing to do," said my mother briskly. "It does people good to get out of the house, and it's better for them to come to the service than stay at home."

It was an interesting argument; the synagogue as mental therapy.

But it didn't seem to work for me. The times I gave in and went with my parents, I often came home morose and angry. They weren't in the least interested in hearing why I didn't want to go. As long as I went, that was good enough.

In adolescence, too, my attitude toward the Sabbath day of rest underwent a significant change.

It's a day designed by middle-aged rabbis for other middle-aged people to enjoy. You go to synagogue, you have a meal, you have a rest, you sit around, you take a nap, you have a snack, you read, you have supper, and then it's over.

That's not what I wanted when I was fifteen. I wanted to visit my friends, not only those within walking distance.

In Israel, the less religious Jews celebrate the day with the activities they choose to observe. They swim, they hike, they visit friends, they travel to the beach or the country, they enjoy hobbies like painting or tennis.

Orthodox Jews refuse to recognize a diversity of interests. In their view, the Sabbath must be a regimented day observed in the way that they feel is right. They throw stones at cars passing through areas where they live on the Sabbath, as if that was a responsible and honorable way to behave. (Less religious Jews are tolerant enough not to throw stones at Orthodox Jews on their way to pray.) The Orthodox denounce any activity of which they disapprove which takes place on the Sabbath because it is not what they want to do.

As a child growing up, I was torn between the two worlds. On the one hand, I hated the long dragging Shabbat afternoons when I wanted to go out, to be active. And on the other, I did not want to hurt my parents or their way of life. And I also felt an enormous burden of guilt, feeling that taking a train or bus on the Sabbath meant breaking the law and must be as serious as murder or stealing.

I felt a disturbing sense of alienation. Why couldn't I accept what was being offered? Why couldn't I believe in it all the way I used to do? Why couldn't I simply let things happen and not keep thinking they were wrong? Why was I the only person in the whole word who didn't fit in?

The Mixed Dancing Sin

I wasn't completely alone. I had a few girl friends within the community who also felt the rules were foolish, and that the time had come for change. But the strength of the wall of opposition was so strong that there was no way we felt we could effect anything of significance.

I knew I could either be a hypocrite, and go on observing and behaving and doing as I had always done, even though I no longer felt there was any good reason for many of the rules. Or I could stop and probably leave.

I never considered the possibility that I would be unable to fit back into the mold once I'd realized what I didn't want. It's like putting aside a favorite shirt or sweater, because it's not quite right for now. When you come to look at it again, it's absolutely wrong and you wonder what on earth made you like it in the first place.

I remember one incident from those early days of re-thinking and reassessment which seemed to typify the attitudes I wanted to reject.

My friends and I belonged to a youth group, which met on Saturday afternoons at the synagogue. It was a very serious group. We'd discuss current events, talk about Israel, sing Hebrew folksongs, and often end our meetings with Israeli folk dances.

There were 20 or so members, boys and girls, all Orthodox but part of the wider society which modern Orthodoxy accepts.

One young man was more religiously observant than the rest of us. He was pleasant, friendly, popular—and clearly moving more and more towards ultra-Orthodoxy. One day he brought up the topic of mixed dancing—when men and women dance together.

"If we are a religious organization, we shouldn't have mixed dancing," he said, seriously, "because it is against the law."

He cited us the Jewish law which said women should not dance with men.

The girls were more indignant than the boys. What was wrong with the Israeli folk dances we did, which were often performed in a circle and rarely involved the kind of close embraces of ballroom dancing? How could he object to something which was part of the heritage of Israel?

He persisted. He said that it was not right for us to dance together. Maybe we could have separate dancing. Maybe we should stop the dancing altogether. We couldn't come to an agreement. We dropped it that day. But he brought it up another time. We rarely danced now at the end of meetings, since we were all self-conscious about the relationships.

I was amazed at the seriousness with which the topic was being discussed. It seemed to me foolish to even consider that it was wrong to dance together. But I misjudged the deep guilt that the young man was exploiting. He had made us feel that we were not behaving like Really Good Orthodox Jews but like Everyone Else.

Finally, he asked for a vote. Looking back on it now, he must have realized I had spoken out against him. As he took the vote, he began at the other end of the group, moving round, looking at each individual. To my surprise, it was a unanimous vote to stop mixed dancing, as hand after hand went up. When he came to me, I hesitated. I was too young to have the courage to stand alone against the group. I didn't know then that he must have understood that. I raised my hand, looking at him as I did so. And I hated him for what he had done to an innocent group of young people, making us feel we were doing something wrong.

I didn't feel I was that different from everyone else. But I felt that I could no longer stifle my own ideas and feelings in order to conform to the majority. I did not want my every action to be approved by majority vote. I wanted to assert my own individuality, to do what I wanted to do, express what I wanted to say, think what I wanted to think without prior censorship by the Rules of Ultra-Orthodoxy. And I objected to the way females were treated.

Of course, I didn't do anything dramatic, immediate or

earth-shattering. I was a self-conscious teenager with acne, long thin legs and untidy hair. I wore glasses and talked too quickly and had been accused of "looking like a Shiksa," the insulting Yiddish word for a non-Jewish woman which is always used by the Orthodox. It was difficult enough wondering if I would ever grow enough to merit a bra, or if anyone would ever love me, or if my hair would ever curl right. I was not ready for a major decision about my religious beliefs.

The Doctrine of Anti-Goyism

The final turning point for me was anti-Goyism.

The mark of a truly devout Hasidic or Orthodox Jew, as well as many other Jews, is an unquestioned hatred of non-Jews. This is the foundation of the ultra-Orthodox and Hasidic philosophy. It's as tenacious, unreasoned and impossible as anti-Semitism, racism and sexism. And as intractable.

What it says is that all non-Jews, or Goyim as the word is in Yiddish since it's the plural of "Goy," are wicked, evil and untrustworthy.

There's a complete litany of all the terrible things about non-Jews which apply to every single one and which are believed implicitly by the Orthodox. These include:

—all Goyim drink alcohol and are always drunk;
—all Goyim are on drugs;
—all Goyim hate Jews even when they seem to be friendly;
—all Goyim are anti-Semites, no matter what they say or do;
—all Goyim have a terrible family life and mistreat their wives and children;
—all Goyim eat pork all the time;
—Goyim are never as clever, as kind, as wise or as honest as Jews;
—you can never ever trust Goyim.

There's much more. But the essence of anti-Goyism is passed to Jewish children with their mother's milk, and then nurtured, fed and watered carefully into a full-blown phobia throughout their lives.

In order to avoid being contaminated by these terrible creatures, the ultra-Orthodox go out of their way to avoid them. Children are taught not to speak to Goyim, not make friends with Goyim, and certainly not have them over to the house.

Those children who go to religious schools and live in the ghetto environment of a closed Orthodox community probably manage to grow up without seeing one of these dangerous people close up. Their attitudes are then perfectly formed. They know whom to hate.

But for most of us growing up in this modern world, it's clear that the unreasoned hatred of a majority group is completely unrealistic. It's hard to ignore the fact that the reason we have running water and electricity in the house is because someone who most likely wasn't an Orthodox Jew built them in for us. And the reason the systems work is because people who are equally likely not Orthodox Jews keep them working.

If you take a train or a bus, it's likely that the driver is not an Orthodox Jew. And if you go to a hospital it's likely you'll be looked after by people who are not Orthodox Jews.

Once you have bridged the gap between myth and reality, you can't go back to believing the fairy tales.

It's like the aftermath of the sweeping integration of black and white schools which has taken place in the United States.

A teacher said after her first weeks of teaching a class of black and white children:

"You don't see the color difference—you just see a classroom of children, each one different from the other."

But the Orthodox fear that attitude. They want their children to hate the Goyim. They don't understand that in a shrinking and diverse world (unlike the empty deserts of the past) it is crucial for people of all beliefs to be able to talk and share and understand each other. They want to deny the humanity that links all people and concentrate on the mythical differences that make them feel superior to everyone else. They are happy to ignore the Outside, and pretend it doesn't exist. They've turned their backs on the world, and they don't want to be part of it because they're sure they're right.

I couldn't accept that blindness. I felt that the bigotry they always blamed on those who said anything negative about Jews was equally visible on the other side of the fence. It seemed to me perfectly crazy to state that all Goyim were thieves, and then to put your money into a bank run entirely by them. It seemed to me ridiculous to state that all Goyim were liars, and then go to a non-Jewish optician who examined your eyes and prescribed glasses which improved your vision. It seemed schizophrenic to say that all Goyim cheated Jews and then buy clothes from stores they owned, because their clothes were better than those in some Jewish-owned stores. It's like the children's game when they show you a picture and ask you to spot what's wrong with it.

I understood anti-Semitism. I'd seen rude slogans about Jews painted on a wall. I understood that some people hated the Jews. But I knew this did not mean All Goyim Everywhere.

In my newly found liberalism, I tried to point this out to my parents.

They certainly didn't want to listen to this heresy.

"You'll see, you'll find out!" shouted my mother, after some twenty years of living in the community without getting to know a single non-Jewish person, even her neighbors.

My father merely shook his head, and said; "You don't understand the history of the Jewish people—look at the history."

But I have looked at the history. And at other histories too. There are periods of persecution, and periods of great safety and security. And there are many other people in the world who suffer when the Jews suffer, and who are persecuted because of their beliefs and faith.

From my perspective, the reason Jews survive is because sympathetic Goyim offer them help. After the Spanish Inquisition of the 1500s, many Jews fled to Holland where a sympathetic Protestant leadership offered them sanctuary. The reason Anne Frank lived so long hidden away in a tiny Dutch attic was because Goyim risked their own lives and safety to protect her and her family from the Nazis. And the reason many survivors of anti-Jewish sentiment are here to tell of their sufferings is because Goyim together with Jews worked to save them.

Anti-Goyism is a foundation of the Orthodox and Hasidic philosophy and way of life. It's so deeply ingrained that even to say something nice about a non-Jew is suspect. To mention that you meet with non-Jews, talk to non-Jews or even have friends among non-Jews is like telling a Klu Klux Klan meeting that you have some black friends.

A friend told me how he was walking home late from work in New York when he saw a Hasidic woman, scarf round her head, long skirt, stockings, walking toward him, looking worried and clearly lost.

"She saw me coming, and you could see the panic in her face," he said. "She didn't know where she was, and yet she didn't dare speak to me as a man, and a non-Jew too."

He decided to take the initiative and asked politely if he could help her.

Terrified, she blurted out that she had taken the wrong subway, and needed to find the way back to Brooklyn. He told her the way to the right subway station, and she hurried off.

"I felt so sorry for her," he said. "She had no idea how to cope with what had happened because she didn't dare to break the rules. And yet she didn't know what to do or where she was."

I wonder what she told her husband when she came home.

The End of the Security Blanket

The years of adolescence broke through the warm protective blanket which covered me completely in my childhood. It's a wonderfully fulfilling sense of security to be part of a tight community where you know everyone believes the same, thinks the same and behaves the same way. And there's the added glue of togetherness in knowing that you are united in a life which is often threatened by the Outside World.

The trouble with thinking about the details of this cozy little ghetto was that I could see it demanded a total suspension of reality. You had to believe all kinds of fairy stories in order to remain secure. You had to ignore whole areas of modern experience in order to hold tight to your out-dated observances. And you had to swallow the most far-fetched of explanations in order to continue behaving in ways which ran counter to modern knowledge and awareness.

If I had been a young boy, I might have accepted the inconsistencies for the sake of the fulfillment and honors I received within the faith. If I had been less adventurous and had not spent my early years with my feisty grandmother, I might have believed that women were helpless and inferior. And if I had been sent to a narrow-minded Orthodox school, I might have been too ignorant to understand what was happening.

But I was a young girl. I had learned that women could cope beautifully when left on their own. And I saw the narrowness of Orthodox Jewish life as a straitjacket of repression for girls and women.

I could see quite clearly from the older girls in the community what lay ahead. Most of them trained as secretaries, and found jobs in Jewish organizations or Jewish-owned businesses. Then they became engaged, and then they had an enormous wedding, and then they "Settled Down," to the subservient life of an Orthodox Jewish Woman.

It didn't seem to me that it would be a lot of fun. There must be more to life than eternal sessions of cooking and cleaning, I thought. I wanted to see the world. I wanted a job that challenged my intelligence. I wanted to meet new people and see new places and experience the variety and diversity of existence. And if I met a man and wanted to marry him, he would have to accept the fact that I didn't want to settle down, keep house, and have dozens of babies.

From what I could see, such ideas never entered the heads of the well-meaning young Orthodox Jewish boys I met in the community. How could you keep the Sabbath if you went travelling around the world? Where would you be sure of finding kosher food? How could you light the candles on Friday nights? What would you do if you could not find a synagogue? And how can a woman do that on her own without a husband?

The turbulence of adolescence sowed the seeds. I knew I couldn't accept the Orthodoxy I had learned. But how could I escape? And what could I do for myself to survive?

I tried hard to imagine what it would be like if I managed to find somewhere that I could live my life the way I wanted to. I tried hard to picture what I would do if I could give up these foolish observances to behave in a more rational and independent fashion. And I tried hard to think through where I was going if I renounced my religion, which I had believed in without a second's doubt throughout my childhood.

It was frightening to realize I didn't believe in it anymore. I tried to make myself go back and accept the things I had always been able to do without question. I tried to pretend I hadn't thought of all the objections and criticisms that flooded my mind.

But there were too many torn spots in the once-perfect fabric for me to be able to stitch it back together again. I could see through the holes and the slits to a distant light of new knowledge and brighter opportunities. I could glimpse somewhere in the future a path which I thought promised me greater happiness and satisfaction than huddling behind the curtains of Orthodoxy.

I knew I had no alternative. I couldn't go back and pretend everything was the way it used to be. I had to go on, believing that if I followed what I hoped was the right way for me, I would eventually reach some kind of destination.

7

Marriage: Meeting, Marrying, and Everyday Troubles

Marriage is the only acceptable status for a Jewish adult, woman or man. The Code of Jewish Law expresses it clearly;

"It is the duty of every man to take a wife to himself, in order to fulfil the precept of propagation. The precept becomes obligatory on a man as soon as he reaches the age of 18. At any rate, no man should pass his twentieth year without taking a wife."

There is one reason, however, for which a man may delay that step: "Only in the event when one is deeply engrossed in the study of the Torah, and he is afraid that marriage might interfere with his studies, may he delay marrying, providing he is not lustful."

I wonder who checks the rate of lustfulness.

For women, the pressures to marry are insistent, because there is no other role suggested to them, not even intense study of the Torah.

How are new Orthodox and Hasidic families created? How do young people meet and mate? What are the Biblical laws about the practices? And what do people do today?

Traditionally, parents organized marriages as a business

arrangement between two sets of families, an accepted way of bringing together young people in many parts of the world. The couple might meet briefly for a formal engagement, but would often see each other for the first time at the wedding ceremony, during which the bride is veiled.

The Bible story shows exactly what might happen with this kind of arrangement. Jacob fell in love with Laban's daughter Rachel, and wanted to marry her. Laban persuaded him to work for Laban for seven years, and after that he would have earned enough money to marry and support her. Jacob did so. But Laban tricked him. He sent his elder daughter, Leah, to sleep with Jacob, and Jacob found he had married a woman he didn't like at all.

Laban then told him that if he worked another seven years, he would be able to marry Rachel as well. So that's what Jacob did, and this time he was given Rachel as his second wife. Laban, meanwhile, had had fourteen years of Jacob's devoted service.

Today, parents still arrange some marriages, introducing his son to her daughter. There's also the "arranger," or "shadchen," a man or woman known in the community for bringing couples together for marriage. Only in less Orthodox groups do young people meet at synagogue celebrations, study sessions, parties, or other events.

A friend told me of a young man in Brooklyn who had become an extra-devout "born again" Orthodox Jew. He told his parents, who were not at all observant, that he wanted to marry a very religious girl, and asked if they would arrange the marriage.

The father, furious, shouted: "I refuse! We are living in the twentieth century! I refuse to allow you to return to the idiot ways of the *shtetl* [village] which we escaped!"

The son, determined, found a "shadchen," and was introduced to a girl. After the first meeting, he confessed to his father that he didn't think she was quite right for him. But he met her twice more.

After the third meeting, he was asked when the engagement should be announced. The young man hesitated, and then said: "I don't want to marry this girl."

There was shock and disbelief. Although it's supposed to be a choice, once a man has taken the first step, it's assumed the wedding is inevitable. Phone calls came from the "shadchen," and from the girl's parents. But he stood firm. Now he is in the imperfect state of being single again, and hopes to try and meet another girl soon.

People may say, "Well, arranged marriages may be as good as any other kind. At least, men and women don't play around. They stay together for years. Isn't that enough?"

There's certainly nothing wrong with bringing together a man and a woman, and hoping that they will marry and find happiness. What's wrong with the Orthodox approach is that the scales are weighted so heavily against the woman. Once she marries, she has no rights and no independence. Should she be mistreated, there is nowhere she can go. And should her husband leave her, she is helpless.

Even in adulterous situations, only women are penalized for their actions. In Biblical times, when a woman was suspected of being unfaithful, she was forced to undergo an ordeal in which she was cursed by a priest and then made to drink water into which he put "the dust that is on the floor of the tabernacle." This ritual, called "sotah," was based on the same concept as the witch-hunts of later years: if the woman was guilty, she would suffer ill-effects; and if she did not, she was innocent.

There is no punishment in Jewish law for a man involved in an act of adultery.

"Once again," notes Rabbi Sally Preisand in her book, *Judaism and the New Woman*, "women were singled out and humiliated in the eyes of the community."

The Wedding Ceremony

Let's assume that our devout young man managed to find a woman who was acceptable and agreed to get married. From the moment the engagement is announced, there are strict rules about separation. On the wedding day itself, the bride and groom are expected to fast as a sign of atonement. The groom may choose to wear a short white gown called a "kittle" as a sign of repentance, since that is what is worn in death, or sometimes on solemn occasions like the Day of Atonement.

The Orthodox marriage is a time for the signing of the contract, which in the past showed that the groom was buying the bride as his property.

Even today, the contract, or "Ketuba," which is read during Orthodox and Hasidic ceremonies, reinforces the old ideas. It contains several clauses, like an official legal document.

After an opening paragraph specifying the date and the day in the Hebrew calendar, and the name of the groom, his father, and the "virgin' (as she's referred to) and her father, the groom says:

"Be my wife according to the practice of Moses and Israel, and I will cherish, honor, support and maintain you in accordance with the custom of Jewish husbands who cherish, honor, support and maintain their wives faithfully. And I here present you with the marriage gift of virgins, two hundred silver zuzim, which belongs to you, according to the law of Moses and Israel; and I will give you your food, clothing and necessities and live with you as husband and wife according to universal custom."

The contract continues that the virgin agrees and that "the trousseau that she brought to him from her father's house in silver, gold, valuables, clothing, furniture, and bedclothes, all this the bridegroom accepted in the sum of one hundred silver pieces, and he consented to increase this amount from his own property with the sum of one hundred silver pieces, making in all two hundred silver pieces."

The contract concludes with the groom affirming that he will pay for the marriage contract and "all my property, even the shirt from my back, shall be mortgaged to secure the payment of the marriage contract, of the trousseau and of the addition made to it." Then it's signed and attested to by two witnesses.

A document like that might have had some validity in an age when women were bought and sold like slaves. But in an era when women are educated, own property or have professional standing in their own right, it's ludicrous.

Today, there are plenty of new contracts of agreement between men and women who are sharing their lives, which
reflect the realities of the experience and which recognize
the rights of women.

And there are also new "Ketubot" which have been written
for use in non-Orthodox ceremonies where men and women
appreciate the progress we've made since the days when
women were of no more concern than sheep.

But if you go to an Orthodox or Hasidic wedding, those
are the words which will be read by the rabbi during the service.

During an extreme Orthodox ceremony, the actual wedding will be the only time the bride and groom are together.
After the blessings have been pronounced, and she has cir-
cled him seven times, he gives her a ring. Then they spend a
brief time together, which in ancient times was the moment
for the consummation of the relationship. Afterwards she
goes with the women and he joins the men for the party and
celebration.

There may be two separate rooms or a partition down the
room. But the separation is essential.

The law is quite specific and even explains why the division
is essential during a wedding celebration:

"Care must be taken that men and women should not eat
in the same room . . .because there is no joy where the Evil
Impulse reigns," states the Code of Jewish Law.

The grace after meals is sung by the men. The dancing, if
there is any, is done with men dancing with men and women
with women. One commentator notes that it is acceptable for
the rabbi to dance and entertain the women on this occasion.
(I wonder what the women think about that.)

The moment of truth for the bride and groom comes
when they finally leave the party and go to spend their first
night together. They must be like any other innocent couple,
strangers to each other, and virgins, presumably. Their
knowledge of sex is limited, since it's forbidden in their upbringing. Even masturbation is sternly forbidden.

I suppose that if they were truly Orthodox they would already have arranged for a proper sheet to be on the bed.

The laws of Orthodox cohabitation demand complete modesty. A man must never see his wife undressed. So when they actually arrive in bed, the idea is to keep her covered by the sheet at all times. However, since propagation is essential, and decreed by law, there's a hole at the appropriate place so that the commandments can be fulfilled.

The wedding night experience is probably as unsatisfying and unexpected as it is during the first time of lovemaking for any other couple completely uninformed about what is involved. It would be comforting to believe that people know how to do these things automatically, and no one has to be told. But as sex therapists and doctors learn from their observations, ignorance does not lead to bliss.

Sexual fulfillment comes with experience and with time. The essential approach of Orthodoxy is to demand performance, and procreation.

The Orthodox wedding epitomizes the attitudes toward women to be found in the ceremony. The mother is not even mentioned in the "Ketuba" listing. The celebrations separate men and women. And the chance for getting to know each other, for time together or for a relationship based on a sense of mutual equality, is minimal.

I found a very different experience when I attended the wedding of a friend's daughter. It felt as if I had moved centuries ahead in time from the atmosphere of Orthodoxy in which I had grown up, and the extremist Orthodox groups so active today.

The family belongs to a Reform synagogue, where my friend has served as a marriage guidance counselor in their community program. Her husband is a physician.

The eldest daughter, Amanda, works in an advertising agency. She met Lionel, a graphic designer and artist. They went out together for some time, and then decided to live together. Now, in their mid-twenties, they agreed to marry.

At the synagogue ceremony, the service was held under the traditional canopy. Both men and women sat together, not separated by a screen. The rabbi in the service mentioned both fathers and mothers, as well as the involvement of my friend in synagogue activities. The bride and groom exchanged rings, and mutual affirmations of love and support.

Afterwards, men and women sat together during the celebration, the bride with the groom, her mother next to her father. Friends and relatives relaxed in the atmosphere.

In an unusual step, the bride's mother made a speech:

"I want to thank three women who have made my daughter's life so special and given her three wonderful role models to follow."

She mentioned her own mother, the groom's grandmother, and his mother, who had recently died. It was an affirmation of the courage and dedication of women, a moving sharing of emotion by a mother with her daughter at a wedding. How different from the male monopoly so evident in Orthodoxy!

Sexual Attitudes

The Bible and Judaic interpretations have never been prudish about sex. The Code of Jewish Law has chapters of rules and regulations about "Laws Concerning Marriage," "The Sin of Discharging Semen in Vain," "Laws of Chastity" and "Prenuptial Laws."

Every detail has been carefully considered. For example: "A man should accustom himself to be in a mood of supreme holiness and to have pure thoughts when having intercourse. He should not indulge in levity with his wife, nor defile his mouth with indecent jests, even in private conversation with her. . . . He should not converse with her either at copulation or immediately before it, excepting about matters directly needed for the act. . . . The intercourse should be in the most modest manner possible. He underneath and she above him is considered an impudent act; both at the same level is considered a perverted act. It is told of Rabbi Eliezer that he used to have cohabitation with such awe and terror that it appeared as if a demon was forcing him to do it."

I presume the author of the Code thought that Rabbi Eliezer was showing exemplary behavior in his reactions.

Then the laws decree what to think about.

"When having intercourse, one should think of some subjects of the Torah, or of some other sacred subjects. . . . His intention should be not to satisfy his personal desire, but to perform his marital duty, like one paying a debt. . . . It is also proper to think of improving the embryo."

It's a wonder any procreation takes place at all with so much to concentrate on.

Of course this is all taking place in total darkness.

"It is forbidden to have intercourse by a light, even if the light is shut out by means of a garment; but it is permissible if one makes a partition, ten hand-breadths (forty inches) high in front of the light. . . . At night if the moon shines directly upon them, it is forbidden, but if it does not shine directly upon them it is permissible if that light is shut out by a garment."

And again, men are told when to have intercourse.

"If possible, a man should be careful not to have cohabitation either at the beginning or at the end of the night, but in the middle."

And where:

"It is forbidden to have cohabitation in the market places, in streets, in gardens, or in orchards; it is permitted in dwellings only, so that it may not resemble fornication."

But assuming the dutiful man follows all the rules, and obeys all the injunctions in the Code of Jewish Law, and studies all the rabbinic comments about cohabitation, or sex, as it's more commonly known, he still won't be able to qualify as a Really Good Jew.

Because like most religious leaders, the rabbis didn't really encourage sexuality, and cautioned sternly:

"He who indulges in having intercourse, ages quickly, his strength ebbs, his eyes grow dim, his breath becomes foul, the hair of his head, eyelashes and brows fall out, the hair of his beard, armpits and feet increase, his teeth fall out, and many other aches besides these befall him," asserts the Code of Jewish Law. What's more, say the authorities sounding more cautionary advice:

"Great physicians said that one out of a thousand dies from other diseases, while nine hundred and ninety-nine die from sexual indulgence."

Now I wonder where that study came from. Where did they dig up statistics as compelling and as dramatic as those? Who were the "great physicians" so easily found and so succinctly quoted?

The statistics I've seen show that times have indeed changed. Today, heart disease, natural accidents, and illness figure prominently on lists of causes of death.

But the rabbinate were never too concerned about explaining their reasons or answering uncomfortable questions related to facts. Rumor, gossip and hearsay guided them. Who needs to ask any more than that? And how can you question a body of law so encumbered by its commentaries that the original sources have long been forgotten?

The Reality of Marriage

The majority of rules and regulations about married life don't relate to sex. Orthodox Judaism plans to regulate every minute, every action and every thought of life, and most of that centers in the home.

The newly married Jewish woman finds herself surrounded on all sides by laws and stipulations about what she can do, what her husband can do, what her children can do, what she can cook, buy, eat and wear and what prayers and observances she must make.

Let us now look at the strains of daily life within the confines of the Orthodox demands.

Kosher Kraziness

Every Jewish woman who has tried to live by the Orthodox laws of "kosher" food regulations knows that they were invented by men.

The essence of the Biblical injunction for one set of rules is simple: "Do not boil a kid in its mother's milk." Sounds pretty straightforward to me. You have a baby beef and you don't boil it in the milk you've just taken from its mother.

The rabbis however jumped on this verse as if it contained the secrets of nutrition. From this they decided:

—meat dishes and milk dishes must be completely separated;
—meat meals and milk meals must be quite separate;
—you have to wait a certain number of hours after eating meat before you have milk, lest you mix the two up inside;
—you have to wait a short while after drinking milk before you have meat for the same reason.

In case you think this prohibition has relaxed over the years, watch the expression on a waiter's face in a "kosher" restaurant if you ask for a glass of milk with your hot pastrami sandwich. He may even go into cardiac arrest on the spot.

There are also laws about not eating the blood of an animal. For meat to be properly "kosher" it is soaked in water and salt for a specific length of time before cooking.

There are also definite prohibitions against banned foods. These include pork, which is also banned in the Muslim religion, and shellfish. The only fish permitted is that with scales and gills.

The beef which may be eaten has to be killed while still conscious, by a specific cut of the knife, as described by the Torah. Beef killed any other way is not "kosher" and may not be eaten.

This has resulted in financial benefit to those butchers who sell properly killed beef, which is given a special label, and for which prices are usually higher. It's no different from the now repealed Catholic ruling that fish must be eaten on Fridays, which dates back to medieval times when the fishermen needed to encourage people to buy their product.

Chickens are supposed to be "kosher" too, though I have never been able to understand how a chicken could be anything else. They simply cost more at a "kosher" butcher.

In childhood, I can remember the occasional fiery sermons the minister would launch on the Sabbath, attacking the avarice of certain butchers who were inflating their prices for the "kosher" products they sold, particularly around Jewish holidays. He would berate them roundly for exploiting the congregation, and one or two would look down and avoid his eyes. Afterwards, over lunch, my parents would say how terrible it was that such things happened.

The Jews are not alone in demanding dietary regulations for those who observe its laws. But the burden of observing the laws falls entirely on the women. Few men involve themselves in the daily household tasks of shopping and cleaning in a traditional Orthodox household.

It's the woman who has to find the right store, the right butcher and the right products to ensure that her family is observing the laws about what to eat.

However, not content with making sure she has to keep separate dishes for meat and for milk, the rabbis came up with the concept of "pareve."

"Pareve" is always translated as "either-or." That means that the product is acceptable at a meat meal or a milk meal. It applies to an oddly assorted selection of things, like the non-dairy creamer to put in coffee, the non-milk ice cream, and any utensils or wares made out of glass or see-through materials. It also includes fruit, vegetables and grains, and most other products that aren't milk or meat.

Orthodox Jews divide food up into three categories: there's "milchig," Yiddish for milk; there's "fleischig," Yiddish for meat; and there's "pareve," the adaptable either-or. Everything fits into one of these divisions.

Adhering to laws like these demands an obsessive passion for illogicality. Why, if you live in a place like Maine with shellfish and seafood of every description, should you not take advantage of what's available? Because when the Jews were wandering around the desert on the way to the Promised Land, there weren't any shellfish and so it was wise to be very suspicious of any which were offered after long journeys over hot, dusty lands.

Why can't you have a glass of milk with a meat meal? What is so terrible about this mixture? Here the rabbis go off on several long tangents, bringing in many pseudo-scientific and health theories. But in the end, the only answer is: because the Bible says so.

And what is so unacceptable about pork? That brings up emotional and psychological responses, none of them rooted in any particular logic. There are infections from diseased uncooked pork, but there are dangers from any unclean food. I've never thought cows were much cleaner than pigs, but we drink the milk which comes straight from their udders.

The intense preoccupation with what may and may not be eaten is a compelling diversion from the basic thinking behind such laws, which was to separate the Jews from other people. It prohibited the kind of friendly camaraderie which springs up when you share a meal with another person at their table, or by their campfire, or in their castle. Jews were perpetually suspicious about what they might be served, and in self-protection, cut themselves off from the communities around them.

Dietary laws have gained increased attention over the years. For whatever reasons, what you eat has become much more important as a judge of religiosity than your ethical behavior.

Today, it's much more significant to discuss the details of how "kosher" the kitchen is in judging the character of an Orthodox Jewish neighbor than in considering her kindness or generosity.

A recent article in *The New York Times* focussed on an Orthodox Hasidic family, from the woman's point of view. The photograph showed a woman, robustly smiling, as she stood in her suburban kitchen. It was equipped with:

—two ovens,
—two stovetops,
—two dish washers,
—three sinks.

That's quite an arsenal of apparatus for a family of five. But if you believe in the sanctity of the Jewish laws about keeping "kosher," it all sounds perfectly logical.

Two ovens: essential because one is for meat and one for milk.

Two stovetops: once again, you have to separate things.

Two dishwashers; you certainly have to wash them separately, or heaven forbid, a piece of dirty meat might bump into a slab of half-eaten butter.

Three sinks: well, this is a little more complicated. But you need one for meat, one for milk, and one for "pareve," the either-or category.

Ideally, you could make a case for three of everything. She may even have had two refrigerators, though they weren't mentioned.

Do you realize that this smiling lady has twice as much to clean in her super-double-duper kitchen?

I've even read of people who set up two kitchens so they could be quite sure there wouldn't be any confusion, and not even the aroma of a piece of meat could slip into the milk.

Though the rabbis didn't imagine this kind of duplication, there's no stopping the truly dedicated devotees once they start trying to be even more devout.

One of the great joys of my escape from that obsessive devotion has been the chance to develop my own style of cooking and housekeeping. The freedom is superbly satisfying. Not only have I been able to eat the kind of food I want, but I've shared the burden of the work. My son, daughter and husband have all become proficient in the kitchen and the supermarket. They've learned to cope with the kind of chores long-suffering Jewish mothers are always burdened with, like the true martyrs they were trained to be. And we have all avoided years of needless guilt worrying about what we should not eat.

I can still remember when I was about ten, during the festival of Passover, when you were not allowed to eat anything that might be tainted with bread in any way. That means you have to question everything you normally eat.

A friend and I were walking back from school, two well-brought-up Orthodox Jewish girls. We had just bought a roll of candies from a store. We walked up the hill, and we ate them as we talked.

Suddenly she said to me: "Should we be eating these? Are they 'kosher' for Passover?"

We looked anxiously at the packet. It didn't say anything at all, and it didn't have that special label blessing the candies as acceptable for Passover.

We stood there, feeling horrified and guilty. Had we committed a terrible sin by eating food that wasn't permitted during Passover? What could we do?

We finally agreed to say nothing, and threw away the rest of the candies.

To this day, I can still remember the sense of guilt and fear that struck us, for absolutely no reason at all. There was no chance that the candies were in any way tainted. But we had been brought up to feel so aware of the dangerous possibilities that our logic was suspended. We both believed that we had done something terribly wrong.

We had been "kosher" brain-washed.

Special Effects: The Sabbath Day of Double Work

The idea of a day of rest, first broached in the Ten Commandments, is a wonderful concept. It's a day when everyone can relax, and regular work is put aside.

But for the Orthodox Jewish woman, it simply means that you do twice as much work on Friday, the day before the Jewish Sabbath, so you can have a little break on Saturday.

The rabbis, for example, ruled that there should be no cooking on the Sabbath. That sounds like a great relief for the overworked housewife, especially if the whole family can go out to eat at a good restaurant.

But no, it doesn't mean that. It just means that on the day before the Sabbath, the woman of the house has to plan for a delicious Friday evening dinner, and then a good breakfast, and then a cold lunch, and then perhaps a snack or two until a cold dinner at the end of the Sabbath. Sometimes dinner is delayed until after the end of the Sabbath, so she is free to start cooking again.

Everyone still eats as usual. You just get to do all the dishes on Saturday evening.

There's one other aspect of "No Cooking" which shows only too clearly how the rabbis will change rules when it's to their advantage.

The original Talmudic decisions were made in the Middle East where it's hot and sunny most of the time. Later, the Jews found themselves in colder climates. So the rabbis ruled that if a fire was lit before the Sabbath, and it was untouched throughout the day, it was permissible to keep things hot on it.

Clearly, even the rabbis like a bowl of hot soup in the middle of the Russian winter.

But this means additional work for the woman of the house. She is responsible for lighting the stove so that a pot of hot water or a slow-cooking stew or some other provisions will be prepared and allowed to simmer steadily throughout the Sabbath day.

From a woman's point of view, the only way the Sabbath day can be a complete rest is if someone else takes on the burdens of food preparation and child care. The ideal solution would be to eat out, at a restaurant. Naturally, since it is not permitted to spend any money on the Sabbath, the meal would have to be prepaid. And since no transportation is allowed, it would have to be within walking distance.

But somehow I can't imagine any rabbi saying, "Listen, my sages, to this interpretation of the holy Sabbath. From now on, we shall go out for meals and we shall have a trained nurse look after the children for the day, so our wives can rest."

Every Friday is Panic-day for the Orthodox Jewish woman at home. She's cleaning, she's shopping, she's cooking and she's preparing for a full day's meals for the entire family, when they'll all be eating together, and which must all be ready an hour before sundown when the Sabbath day officially begins.

The wonderful image of the woman at the Friday night table with the two candles lit, the two plaited loaves of bread and the bottle of wine is misleadingly peaceful. Her calm demeanor is that of exhaustion. She's made it in time for the Sabbath and she has done EVERYTHING.

In the prayers which are said, there's one particular psalm which is always quoted as reflecting the perfect image of the Jewish woman. It's the one that men always like to point out as the sign of the excellent status of the woman in Judaism.

I've read it recently. I remember reading it in Hebrew and English as a young girl. I didn't like it much then, and now it is patently offensive.

I've always felt it presented a view of what men think women want to hear, without any discussion of what women might actually feel about it. It's like the man who brings home an electric mixer as a gift for his wife, when she really wanted a bouquet of flowers.

PROVERBS 31: *Praise of a Worthy Woman*

A good wife who can find?
  She is far more precious than
    jewels.
The heart of her husband trusts in
    her,
  and he will have no lack of gain.
She does him good, and not harm,
  all the days of her life.
She seeks wool and flax,
  and works with willing hands.
She is like the ships of the mer-
    chant,
  she brings her food from afar.
She rises while it is yet night
  and provides food for her house-
    hold
  and tasks for her maidens.
She considers a field and buys it;
  with the fruit of her hands she
    plants a vineyard.
She girds her loins with strength
  and makes her arms strong.
She perceives that her merchandise
  is profitable.
  Her lamp does not go out at
    night.

She puts her hands to the distaff,
  and her hands hold the spindle.
She opens her hand to the poor,
  and reaches out her hands to the
    needy.
She is not afraid of snow for her
    household
  for all her household are clothed
    in scarlet.
She makes herself coverings
  her clothing is fine linen and
    purple.
Her husband is known in the gates,
  when he sits among the elders of
    the land.
She makes linen garments and sells
    them;
  she delivers girdles to the mer-
    chant.
Strength and dignity are her cloth-
    ing,
  and she laughs at the time to
    come.
She opens her mouth with wisdom,
  and the teaching of kindness is
    on her tongue.
She looks well to the ways of her
    household,
  and does not eat the bread of
    idleness.
Her children rise up and call her
    blessed;
  her husband also, and he praises
    her:
"Many women have done excel-
    lently,
  but you surpass them all."
Charm is deceitful, and beauty is
    vain,
  but a woman who fears the LORD
    is to be praised.
Give her of the fruit of her hands,

and let her works praise her in
the gates.

This lady is working full time, 24 hours a day, seven days a
week. She's out looking for wool and flax, so that she can spin
it, a time-consuming operation. Then she treks off to the distant markets to buy her food at the best prices. She's up before dawn, as most working mothers often are, and feeds everyone.

Then she moves into real estate, buying a field here, and
planting a vineyard. Presumably she does exercises to "gird
her loins with strength"; perhaps that's what happens after
she's planted the vineyard.

She stays up all night, spinning and weaving. And then she
also gives help to the poor, and the needy, the way many
women today help in social causes.

Comes the winter she makes sure everyone is warmly
dressed, and looks after her own clothes too. She is one of
those fashionable women who always wears the right thing at
the right time.

Meanwhile what is her husband doing?

Well, he's well known in the city, where he "sitteth among
the elders of the land."

She meanwhile is making "fine linen, and selleth it, and
delivereth girdles unto the merchant."

Now comes the soft-soap to persuade her that she's wonderful. "Strength and honor are her clothing; and she shall
rejoice in the time to come."

That's the "Pie in the sky when you die" philosophy of
many faiths. Life may be tough but later, girl, it will be great!

Passover Crumb Mania

If Orthodox Jewish women wear themselves out getting
ready for the Sabbath, they drive themselves into a frenzy of
total exhaustion in the annual preparations for the spring
festival of Passover.

This eight-day event celebrates the escape of the Jews
from slavery in Egypt. On the first and second nights the

story of the Exodus is read from the special book, the "Hag-gadah," and special foods are eaten to remind Jews of the sufferings of their ancestors. The "Seder," as it's called, de-mands incredible preparations.

Among Reform communities and in Israel it's accepted that only one Seder is observed, as decreed in the Bible. However, over the centuries the custom grew up of having two nights of Seder, which is now followed outside Israel.

Let me explain the kind of work that has to be undertaken before Passover, as outlined in a little book called *The Jewish Home:*

"The housewife has to organize in advance the prepara-tion of the Passover, although not just a few days ahead as with the Sabbath, but several weeks beforehand. . . . Most women will begin a routine and thorough cleaning of the home four weeks before the Festival."

Then follows six pages outlining the details of what has to be done, including providing new toothbrushes and mugs for the bathroom.

The essence of the attack is to remove any vestige of crumbs—yes, crumbs—that may be found in the house.

Passover is the time when Jews do not eat bread. That's be-cause when the children of Israel fled from Egypt after the ten plagues, the bread they had made in the evening did not have time to rise. So they were left with some flat pieces of unleavened bread. From that incident came the rules about eating the dry, flat Matzoh pieces during the festival of Pass-over. And hot on the heels of that decision came the rabbinic rules and interpretations of how to get rid of every last ves-tige of crumbs which might contaminate the perfectly unleavened Jewish home.

The Code of Jewish Law goes into excruciating detail about how to get rid of any malicious pieces of bread. The highlight of the preparations for the men is the tour of the house with a candle which must be "only one wax candle, not several twisted together, for then it becomes a torch," and which takes place the evening before Passover begins.

The tour, by the men of course, includes "all the rooms

into which leaven might have been lodged, even the cellars, garrets, stores and woodsheds. All those vessels in which leaven has been kept should also be searched."

And in case the women don't understand what is required, the Code notes: "Before the search is made, all these places should be carefully swept and cleansed of leaven."

The chapter has seventeen paragraphs devoted to "Searching for Leaven" with explicit instructions including:

"Every nook and cranny of all places must be searched with the utmost care. We must also search the pockets of our garments as well as those of our children's garments, as leaven is at times placed therein."

What the laws and the advice to women emphasizes is that should a single crumb be allowed to slip through, the whole process of Passover has been ruined.

In all that I've read, I haven't found a single instance of the rabbis or the men actually getting involved in the carrying out of these rabbinic instructions. The impression is that the work will be done, but that sweeping and cleaning and emptying pockets is better done by someone else, while those who wrote the rules merely supervise the operation and check that it's been completed to the ultimate degree of religious perfection.

Orthodox Jewish women go into a frenzy before Passover. It's not like the old days when people lived in simple tents and sweeping the sand out of the entrance was enough. Or the time when Jews made their homes in farmhouses with one large room downstairs and a large sleeping area. Today, in the basic four-bedroom suburban home or the crowded apartment, there could be crumbs *everywhere,* and the apprehension felt by most Jewish women at the approach of Passover is rooted in a deep conviction that they will miss one crumb, and spoil it all.

Here's an outline of what most women expect to do before they sit down at the Passover Seder service on the first evening:

Clean out every room in the house. If you read what the Code of Jewish Law says, would you feel comfortable skipping the woodshed?

Change all the plates, cups, saucers and dishes. Generally, Orthodox families have four sets of dishes:

—one for meat;
—one for milk;
—one for Passover for meat;
—one for Passover for milk.

The Code demands that "all vessels which have not been made ritually fit for Passover should be thoroughly scoured and rinsed in the forenoon before Passover in such a manner that no leaven be visible on them, and then concealed in a place which is not frequented. It is best to lock them up in separate rooms and hide the key until after Passover."

So the dutiful housewife puts away her everyday pots, plates and other dishes, and gets out her Passover dishes. Then she locks up the naughty leavened plates and hides the key. I've never been sure why the plates had to be locked up, since no devout family member would want to touch them, and they are unlikely to move by themselves.

Clear out every piece of unleavened food in the house. This might mean simply throwing out the half-loaf, the hamburger rolls and the cookies. But that is too simple.

In the maniacal devotion to overkill, the Jewish housewife goes berserk. Any product on the shelf—pickles, marmalade, peanut butter, canned peaches, tomato sauce, canned beans and more—might, and I repeat might, be contaminated by leaven. So, just to be on the safe side, Jewish housewives buy scores of replacement products with an itsy-bitsy paper label on which it says "Kosher for Passover." It usually says it in Hebrew, and has an official looking seal of the rabbinate. That's enough to create guilt in a Jewish woman trying to observe out-dated rules.

Now in the old days, when women went to the market and bought their food from open stands where perhaps, unexpectedly, the owner might sprinkle the crumbs from his midday sandwich over the food, there might be some reason for restocking the kitchen shelves.

But in the day of ultra-hygienic sterilized jars and cans,

when it's sometimes impossible to undo the tops, there's no way a piece of leaven could sneak into a jar of strawberry preserves. There is no difference at all between the jar she bought last week and the jar she buys for Passover, except for the itsy-bitsy label. But she believes she's being a Better Jew for buying it.

Prepare the meal and the special dishes for the Seder. The Code of Jewish Law never hesitates to speak out. There are pages on how to bake "matzoh," what wine to choose, what vegetable to use for dipping in the salt water, how to make the paste-like mixture called "haroset," where to arrange the seats at the table, and details like "the wine cups must be whole without a flaw, thoroughly washed, and they must hold no less than one and a half eggshells."

The Jewish woman, exhausted from changing dishes, cleaning house, and sweeping up malingering breadcrumbs, now launches into the preparation of a full-scale meal, usually for guests and family, plus the careful arrangement of the special needs of the services before the meal.

I can remember very well the anxiety with which my mother prepared for Passover. Her temper became shorter, and her work increased as the day drew near for the Seder. My father meanwhile sat at his desk studying the "Haggadah" and preparing for the service. He never lifted a finger to help in the physical work of the preparations. And then he and my brother would gleefully tour the house to inspect for crumbs.

By the time we actually sat down, there was a sense of total exhaustion. *The Jewish Home* book sums it up:

"The wife will sit back, tired but satisfied, knowing that she has carried out every detail of the Passover preparation meticulously."

Over the years I have celebrated Passover Seders in many different places and with different people. In comparing the Orthodox experiences with those held in more relaxed atmospheres, the differences are enormous. The most obvious is that women enjoy non-Orthodox events more.

All the Orthodox women I've met, from my mother and

her friends to the women of my own generation, dread the preparations for Passover. I've never found an Orthodox woman who truly looks forward to all that's involved. And I've never met an Orthodox woman who admits she does nothing at all.

There's an obsession about cleaning, scrubbing and chasing crumbs that is bizarre in the light of all we know about cleanliness. But the insanity is part of the Code of Jewish Law and the Talmudic and rabbinic interpretations. There are pages of explanations on how to sell the unleavened bread in the house to a non-Jew, so that there's no sin if a crumb or two appears. There are discussions on whether it's acceptable to drink the milk from a cow which provides milk the rest of the year. And there are detailed instructions on how to purify vessels for Passover including such items as "a vessel which has been regularly used for keeping brandy does not discharge the odor and taste of the brandy through water-purification. It should be first boiled in water and ashes until its odor is entirely dissipated, and then again immersed in hot water."

It's hard to break a cycle of obsession that has been perpetuated for centuries.

I've tried discussing this with Orthodox friends and find that it's tough.

Tamara is an independent liberated woman, with a master's degree in psychology and a responsible job at a university. Yet I have watched her driving herself to the point of collapse as she gets ready for Passover. When I once suggested that the work was pointless, I was firmly put in my place.

"You don't understand!" she snapped. "This is what is expected, and it's what Mike's mother did for him, and it's what he expects to see, and that's what he wants." She was already worried that she didn't have time to wash the windows and to line all the kitchen cabinets with clean paper.

Another friend grew up in a Reform family, with a warm but relaxed attitude toward Passover. She told me that until she married Irving she had never even known about the rules about getting ready for Passover.

The first year she was so exhausted from the preparations that when I called to wish her a happy celebration her husband told me she had collapsed and gone to bed.

"Why do you do it?" I asked when I spoke to her recently. "You don't have to, you know. Can't you see that you're being manipulated by the ages-old attitudes of rabbis and other men? You object when people take advantage of you at work because you're a woman, but that's just what Jewish laws do."

"Look, it's what Irving wants," she said, "because he tells me about the things his mother did and how he remembers the details, and he really gets such a kick out of it."

"You can give him a wonderful Seder and a beautiful experience without driving yourself into exhaustion," I said.

She sighed. "I know it's crazy. Most years I fall asleep during the Seder because I'm so tired. But this is what you're supposed to do for a really 'kosher' Passover.'"

"He doesn't want to see you worn out completely at the Seder," I said. "He won't even know if you don't change the china and glasses, and what does it matter anyway? And look at what you're teaching your daughters by doing it all yourself and trying to conform to what you think he'd like."

She could only repeat: "It's what Irving wants."

What men want is the keystone of all decisions in the family of the Orthodox.

It's reflected not only in the day-to-day practices of keeping a "kosher" home, or of observing the Sabbath and the Jewish holidays, but also in more serious confrontations.

If a woman feels that her husband is treating her badly, or is behaving unethically, or in any way begins to think that perhaps this marriage is much further from the perfection she once dreamed of than she can accept, there's little she can do. In the eyes of the community, he is always in the right. Even if she considers a separation or a divorce, she is made to feel that she is the wrongdoer.

What About Divorce?

The rabbinate of the Orthodox and Hasidic like to point to the low divorce rate among their families. When divorce was impossible to obtain in the secular world, the rate was low too. But there was a great deal of unhappiness, of violence, of exploitation and of adultery going on which no one ever mentioned publicly.

The only way to compare the stability of families within Orthodoxy and outside is to provide an option for women within marriage if they feel it is imposssible to continue. When a woman knows that complaining about her marriage brings no recognition of the difficulties, she stops complaining. But the cruelty, the thoughtlessness and the selfishness of her husband continues. She has no recourse to help of any kind within Orthodoxy. She cannot imagine life outside the ghetto because she has been carefully deprived of all useful training for coping in the outside world. And she slowly loses her own confidence, her self-esteem, as the years pass.

I've met several divorced modern women. They have made their own lives positive and enriching. They don't have a supportive loving husband, but then, they never had one within the marriage they left. One woman said, "It's still a relief to know that I don't have to keep wondering who he's sleeping around with, and what lie he's going to tell me when he comes home." Today, she is bringing up her three children on her own, has a job as a dental assistant, and lives in a comfortable home.

Orthodoxy likes to pretend that all Orthodox men are perfect. Having met many of them, I know they're only human.

I hate to emphasize this point, but just because a man follows the bizarre routines of the ultra-Orthodox or dresses up in the 18th-century costumes of the Hasidim, it doesn't mean that he is any kinder, more honest or truthful, more generous, more considerate, more loving or more sexually competent than anyone else.

The quantity of good qualities and bad qualities in the universe is unlimited. They are scattered round in random fashion among the peoples of the world. You'll find mean, unkind men among the Orthodox just as you can find them among Conservative Jews. You can find kind, generous people among the Hasidim just as you can find them among Reform Jews.

But within Orthodoxy and Hasidim you know that you'll find an outstanding ignorance about sexuality, about women's rights and about what women can do, which you will only find outside in the extremist fundamentalist Christian and other religious sects.

You'll also find a mind-set fostered by hundreds of years of misplaced religious instruction that places women in a lowly, servile position, unable to cope with the world as men do. And you'll find that Orthodox men have the strangest misconceptions about women as seductresses, as lewd temptresses and as unclean beings which is appalling to recognize in these modern times.

The rabbis have no intention of changing their approach.

Jewish divorce laws discriminate against women. As usual, the man has the right of divorce. In the past a man told his wife he was divorcing her, and drove her out of the house, which he owned. If the woman wanted to marry again, she needed to have a document called a "get" or Bill of Divorce. Her husband did not need one to remarry since he could have more than one wife.

Over the years, the rabbis made changes to protect the rights of the woman. However, in order to obtain a religious divorce, particularly in Israel where the Orthodox rabbinate control all matters of marriage, divorce and family matters, a woman must appear before an all-male board to plead her case. Her husband must agree to sight the "get" or she is not legally divorced according to Jewish law.

There's one serious problem for women under Jewish law which has not yet been resolved. If a woman's husband disappears, deserts her or is missing and presumed dead, she is still considered married without a "get" or definite proof of his death. She is called an "agunah," a deserted woman, and she cannot remarry under any circumstances. This is a tragedy for many women, who are caught in a situation entirely dependent on their ex-husbands' good will. Irwin H. Haut in *Divorce in Jewish Law and Life,* published in 1983, estimates that there are about 15,000 women in New York City in the state of "agunah."

A married woman becomes totally dependent on her husband. The Orthodox, like most other extremist groups, like to pretend that all husbands are perfect and all marriages are made in Heaven. This is not the case. Orthodox men and women are made up of the same amounts of good and bad as other people. They like to pretend that things are different. But the reality keeps surfacing.

For example, some Orthodox men beat their wives. This would never have been admitted publicly by men. But there are now battered wives shelters with strictly "kosher" kitchens for the Orthodox wives who have left the violence of their husbands in desperation.

"To the outside world, the battered Jewish wife and her battering husband appear to be an ideal couple," writes Mimi Scarf, founder and director of a shelter for battered Jewish wives in Los Angeles. "Neither is an alcohol or drug abuser. They belong to a synagogue and their children are being educated there. They attend business functions together and are cordial in public. The husband appears to be a paradigm of gentleness and charm, the perfect husband. One would not be able to guess that there is any difference between his public and private behavior."

From the many case histories she has seen, she knows the realities of the man who pushes his wife out of the car, miles from home, and leaves her, and the man who locks his wife out of the house in her nightclothes.

"In private he criticizes everything she does—cooking, cleaning, entertaining—and he blames her for everything that goes wrong. If a child has an accident, she is not a good mother. If a record player breaks, she broke it. . . . Jewish battered women all report that their husbands are constantly punishing them for something or other."

The only step that ended the beatings, according to the wives, was to threaten to tell the world that it was happening.

"Only when the husband was threatened with public exposure did he cease to brutalize his wife," notes Ms. Scarf, and concludes:

"It is tempting to teach our children that the Jewish family is superior to all others, or that Jewish husbands are above reproach; parents, rabbis, social workers, indeed all who are part of the Jewish community, must be ready to recognize and admit that our idealized concept of the Jewish family is just that: an idealized concept, a myth."

8

The Unclean Wife: What Orthodox Laws Really Teach About Menstruating Women

When I was growing up in the Orthodox Jewish community, I accepted the idea that women could not take part in services or have a Bat Mitzva ceremony because we menstruated, so we were unclean.

I can't pinpoint exactly when that idea fixed itself in my mind. Maybe I absorbed it, by osmosis, from all that I saw around me. But it was one of the things I knew for certain.

There are authorities who say that women are worthy of taking part in services and all the other rites and observances of Judaism. By the time I had grown up, I already understood that I was tainted by being a woman. I can empathize with Orthodox Jewish women who become Reform Jews, and then find it impossible to take part in rituals because of their own excluded upbringing.

In my Hebrew classes, we must have learned something of

the separation of men and women. We certainly would have been considered too young to study the detailed laws about marriage and menstruation. And so I had only a vague idea about the discrimination against women because of their monthly periods.

Before writing this book, I researched the Bible, the separation laws in the code of Jewish Law, and several recently published texts in English on "Family Purity." I was appalled. What I had learned as a child was the tip of the iceberg: the laws are discriminatory and insulting beyond my wildest imaginings.

Instead of asserting that women are capable, strong and admirable human beings who can learn, grow and achieve all that they strive for and be actively involved in every aspect of life, and happen to menstruate, they've come to a different conclusion. They believe that because women menstruate, they therefore are incapable of learning, struggling, achieving or taking part in any aspect of life outside the home, because they are cursed with a monthly cycle of bleeding, and are unclean.

In Susan Weidman Schneider's book *Jewish and Female,* Rabbi Laura Geller comments: "Menstrual taboos are responsible for real damage to Jewish women's views of themselves and their bodies. I have met many women who learned nothing about the Torah except that they could not touch the Torah because they menstruate. . . . Their sense of themselves as 'inferior' Jews has already permeated their relationship to tradition and to their own bodies."

What Orthodox and Hasidic Judaism do is to focus on the "negative" side of women's abilities.

Dr. Mortimer Ostow, who was chairman of the Department of Pastoral Psychology at the Conservative Jewish Theological Seminary, said in a 1974 speech that:

"Menstrual discharge is repulsive. . . . Among the men who will oppose the presence of women on the 'bimah' [altar or platform of a synagogue] will be many who fear that a menstruating woman will contaminate them, and the sacred objects, especially the Torah."

Where the Rules Come From

The idea that women are contaminated by their monthly know of course that the cycle of ovulation and menstruation are interdependent. Many primitive people still do not connect the two events. Judaism, living by precepts set centuries ago, still discriminates against women when they are bleeding and consider them unclean after childbirth.

The reasons for this attitude stem initially from the book of Leviticus. Chapter 14 deals with how the Lord told Moses to treat an outbreak of leprosy, and separate the unclean lepers. Next, Chapter 15 talks of unclean men, what must be done when a man has a discharge from his body, like an emission of semen. Then it moves on to say: "When a woman has a discharge of blood which is her regular discharge from her body, she shall be in her impurity for seven days, and whoever touches her shall be unclean until the evening."

The tone of the approach to the woman is the same as that towards the leper:

"Everything upon which she lies during her impurity shall be unclean; everything upon which she sits shall be unclean. And whoever touches her bed shall wash his clothes, and bathe himself in water, and be unclean until the evening. And whoever touches anything upon which she sits shall wash his clothes and bathe himself in water and be unclean until the evening."

There's no direct mention of the ritual bath or *Mikveh* here. The Bible recommends: "She shall count for herself seven days and after that, she shall be clean."

She is expected to follow the old custom:

"She shall take two turtledoves or two young pigeons and bring them to the priest. . . And the priest shall offer one for a sin offering and one for a burnt offering; and the priest shall make atonement before the Lord for her unclean discharge."

The chapters in this section of Leviticus deal with the gory details of offerings to expiate sin, where people gave the priests live animals and "the priest shall throw its blood against the altar round about."

Over the years, rabbis decided that the laws about such offerings can be ignored. They are part of a tradition which existed when the temple was in existence in Jerusalem, but do not apply today. There are those who believe such customs will return when the temple is rebuilt. But others consider these traditions outdated.

The laws about women's bleeding and how women must be treated as unclean during menstruation date from the same period in history.

The extreme Orthodox and Hasidim still insist women obey the laws about being menstrually unclean, even though these are rooted in exactly the same outdated attitudes. The thinking which demanded blood-stained animal sacrifices also feared the monthly bleeding of women. That led to a fear of contamination, and the strict laws of separation.

These ignorant ideas are still held by primitive societies today.

In the South Pacific, there's a community on the island of Mogmog which has been isolated from the rest of the world because of its geographical location.

Living in simple grass huts, and wearing few clothes, the people have strict rituals relating to menstruating women. When a young girl begins to menstruate, she is sent to the "Ipul" or women's house. The other women there greet her loudly. She stays with them and, like them, may not cook for the men or eat with others for eight days. The women spend their time weaving and talking among themselves.

After the eight days, the women return to their huts.

But even in this outlying outpost, change is coming. The area is now part of the Yap state of Micronesia. Education brings together boys and girls, to end the discriminatory attitudes of the past.

Jewish law exempts women from many of the duties of prayer because of the demands of taking care of the household. She may observe the many commandments if she chooses, but, unlike a man, she is not duty bound to do so.

A woman has three specific obligations: the first, as we have seen, is to light candles on the eve of the Sabbath, on Friday night. The law stipulates that if she neglects to light candles, she must light an extra candle every Friday night as long as she lives.

The second is one dating back to the days when the Temple stood. She must make dough, called *hallah*, and set part of it aside as a sacrifice, which was consecrated to the priests in the Temple. After the Temple had been destroyed more than 2,000 years ago, the custom developed of taking a small piece of dough and throwing it into the fire or oven.

The third duty is to observe the laws of separation, or *niddah*. These laws specify exactly how a woman must conduct herself during the days she is menstruating, and the seven days after her period ends, with details of how she must avoid sexual or physical contact of any kind with her husband until after immersion in a ritual bath.

According to one source, women who abandon the laws of *niddah* will be punished by death in childbirth. Today in Israel, each prospective bride receives a booklet telling her to observe the laws of family purity and repeating that ancient threat, quoting anonymous medical opinions to enforce observance.

Once again, Biblical attitudes have narrowly defined what a woman might do.

She has no role in synagogue services. She has no place in prayers at home. She is unnecessary in most religious ceremonies.

Her only role is to light two candles on a Friday evening, to make dough, and to remember the laws which keep her separate because she is unclean.

What is even more disturbing is that the *niddah* laws promote the mis-titled concept of "Family Purity" and present completely misleading medical information for women about their bodies.

What the Laws Say

The Code of Jewish Law is the basic source of the laws of *niddah* when a woman is separated because she's unclean. In one translation, by Rabbi S. Wagschal, there are 85 pages of rules, regulations and interpretations covering every minute aspect of the menstrual cycle.

As a woman I've had many, many periods. I've talked to many other women of various ages about their periods. I've seen a great many women serving as political leaders, as teachers, as business executives, as social workers, as doctors, as artists and as full time parents. And in every single case, the woman managed to fulfill the role successfully. She also survived her monthly periods without any problems.

There are times when women experience pain. There are times when women feel emotionally tense. There are times when women feel physically tired. But these feelings are not a monopoly of menstruation. They are sometimes related to a period, but often they are part of our total existence. Women's lives are not ruled by menstrual cycles to the exclusion of all other choices, except in the eyes of the Orthodox and Hasidic leaders.

What's more, it wouldn't take me 85 pages to discuss how to cope with menstruation, what to do, and what I feel about it. It's not a complicated issue to describe; it's simply a part of a woman's life between the ages of about 14 and 50.

The rabbis drew up a series of definitions for "Regular Periods" (which follow a regular pattern for at least three consecutive periods) and "Irregular Periods," which they divide up into Lunar Cycles, Same-Interval Cycles and Thirty Day Cycles. They desperately wanted to make sure that women fitted into these categories, and that everything was under control.

What's more, if a woman's period hasn't started when it was supposed to, they discover all kinds of symptoms which they feel are equally significant:

"Some women before menstruation stretch their arms from weariness, or yawn from drowsiness or belch after meals," says the Code of Jewish Law. "If a woman sneezes, or feels a pain in the region of the navel or the womb, or has an attack of chills or fever, or the hair of her body or of her head bristle, or her head or her limbs grow heavy, if any of these symptoms occurs immediately before the menses for three periods in succession, it may serve to establish the date of her menses. This is termed 'menses regulated by physical symptoms.' "

It's certainly a strange system of medical observation to assume that a woman's menstrual flow has begun because she sneezes or yawns. But the rabbis felt sure they were right and they had no intention of changing their opinions, no matter if biology has proven otherwise.

What the laws do is to make a woman overwhelmingly aware of the cycle of her body, and her own sense of powerlessness to control her menstrual bleeding. There's no way a woman can pinpoint exactly when her period will begin every time, no matter how carefully she scrutinizes the calendar or multiplies out the "Lunar Cycle" or the "Same Interval Cycle." What women can do is to focus on positive, self-enhancing and self-rewarding aspects of life so that they feel good about their own abilities, and accept their menstrual cycles as only one part of their lives. The rabbis don't accept that view.

What's more, they go out of their way to detail the way in which a woman must behave during the time of her uncleanliness, so that everyone with whom she comes in contact is aware of her state.

Let's take a look at a few of the specific stipulations about behavior.

The Don't Touch Laws

The Code of Jewish law warns:

"The husband in that period should not touch her, even with his little finger. He is not allowed to hand anything to her, be it even a long object, nor to receive anything from her. Throwing anything from his hand into her hand, or vice versa, is forbidden."

This ban extends even to mealtime. He's not allowed to eat with her at the same table, unless something is put between them on the table. He can't drink what's left in her cup, and she can't pour him out a cup of wine if he's there.

"It is proper for her to wear special clothes during the days of her impurity, so that both of them may remember that she is menstrually unclean," intones the Code.

Beds figure large in the rabbinic concern. A husband and wife are not allowed to sleep in the same bed, even if they both have their clothes on and have separate mattresses. If they choose separate beds, the beds must not touch one another.

If he's sick in bed, she is, however, allowed to look after him. She can even touch him to help him sit up or lie down. But she must not make his bed when he is around.

On the other hand, if she is sick, the husband "is forbidden to attend to her even without touching her."

I can just imagine the poor woman, lying in agony in bed, longing for a little care and attention, but left alone to suffer in her State of Menstrually Unclean.

When she serves the food she has to put it down "in a slightly unusual way—in front of him with her left hand, or set it down slightly away from him."

The workings of the rabbinic mind are bizarre indeed. Here's a hardworking Orthodox or Hasidic Jewish wife, serving a delicious meal she has slaved over one of her hot stoves to make, and when it comes time to serve, she has to do something a little peculiar so that her husband will notice that she's behaving oddly and remember she's menstruating. Maybe he'll just assume she's a bit crazy and ignore the whole thing. It certainly doesn't do much to enhance the intellectual status of the wife.

If I'd been writing these laws, I'd have said that if the wife was "unclean" during this time, she should definitely not touch food or any household appliance. In fact, during this time her husband should do everything for her to make sure that none of the family is contaminated by her. Surely, when someone has leprosy, you don't like them peeling the potatoes or whipping up the noodles or slicing the apples?

There are rules about travelling.

"They should not ride in the same wagon or take a voyage in the same ship, if the trip is made for pleasure, like riding through parks, orchards, or the like," says the Code firmly. "If they travel from one city to another in the course of business, it is permissible, even though they are by themselves, provided they do not touch one another."

Rabbi Wagschal, in his interpretation, has taken the liberty of updating the rules.

"When travelling in a taxi, bus, train or plane, the main concern should be that they sit in such a way that they cannot come in contact," he says in his *Guide to the Laws of Family Purity.* "They may not go together in a rowing or motor boat," he adds, though "a large boat is considered to be like a motor car."

He even regulates what they talk about, stating that "although conversation should be conducted in the usual friendly way, nevertheless they should refrain from intimate or frivolous talk."

They can, of course, discuss the laws about *niddah* separation.

It's almost funny to see a group of earnest religious men trying to force women to organize a perfectly natural human function. It was a ridiculous way to treat Jewish women in the past, and I'm horrified to think of the little Orthodox and Hasidic girls being taught these same ideas in America today.

There are plenty of excellent medical texts available about menstruation, its cycles and its effects. These are based on actual experiences, objective scientific research and observations of real women, sharing what they know to be true.

Most women learn that no period is ever perfectly regular or irregular. It's a part of the pattern of life. An unexpected cold, a strenuous work week, a busy trip, emotional stress, or worry can all affect the cycle. Sometimes a period arrives late, sometimes it comes early. Sometimes it lasts four days, sometimes five, sometimes two, sometimes three. Most women adapt to their own personal cycle and learn to notice deviations if they are extreme. Most women notice when they skip a period. But after a few years, most women accept menstruation as part of everyday life, and focus on other aspects of their existence, instead of fixating on the menstrual experience.

Menstruation is simply part of the reproductive cycle, affecting women for a few days each month with few visible physical effects.

The essence of these picayune laws is to divert attention

from the true enormity of what is happening. A human being, a woman, is treated as if she were untouchable and beneath consideration as a person. For the days of her bleeding, and for the week following that time, she is treated with
the kind of physical disdain and fear usually shown to people
with the plague.

But in the centuries of studying, writing, analyzing and
discussing these laws not one man has ever suggested that
perhaps they should be thrown out, just as the laws about
slaughtering sheep for sacrifices have been dismissed.

Instead, the laws have been embellished and extended, by
century after century of rabbinic interpretation.

I can remember the kind of thinking that went on when
similar topics came up in my Hebrew classes. For instance,
let's look at the situation where a man and a woman are trav-
eling together. Are they able to share a hotel bed if she is
menstruating?

The teacher would present the situation, and throw it
open to the class. There'd be a lively discussion about possible solutions; how she could sleep on the floor and he could
have the bed, or how they could have a spare bed rolled in,
or how he could sleep in the car and she could have the bed.
In my innocence, I'd suggest the topic was ridiculous and
that of course they should both share the bed. My suggestion
would be dismissed. The Orthodox way is to ignore the fundamentals and concentrate on the peripherals.

With an intellectual delight bordering on the maniacal, the
discussion might examine whether they should drive on to
another hotel where they can find two rooms, or whether it
would be better to drive through the night in order to avoid
facing the situation. Or perhaps she could go home by plane
to allow him to have the bed for sleep, and then she could
sleep at home. Would an air mattress on the bed, separated
from it, be acceptable? Could they put the mattress on the
floor and divide it with a piece of wood?

After hundreds of years of rabbinic discussions at this
level, how could any woman stand up and say: "Enough! The
basic law about menstrual separateness is wrong, it no longer
has any validity. It must be abolished forthwith."

The men would stare at her open-mouthed. They would look through the pages of rules and regulations and arguments which have taken place over the years. They would reread the old interpretations and the older interpretations and the oldest interpretations. They would pore over the Talmudic sayings and the myths and the ancient stories. It would be beyond their comprehension to accept the idea that the law itself was wrong.

An understanding rabbi might suggest, "Well, perhaps we can make a few adjustments here and there, because after all, times do change."

So perhaps they'll allow the wife to share a hotel bed, if they both keep all their clothes on. Now that's the kind of dramatic revision which keeps Orthodox and Hasidic rabbis agog with excitement for months.

Is She Clean?

The Code of Jewish Law goes into excruciating detail so that women can make sure their bleeding has ended and that they are almost clean again.

Taking a cloth, "she should inspect both sides of the cloth to ensure that it is perfectly clean," one book advises women. "It is then wrapped around the forefinger and a thorough yet gentle internal examination is made by inserting the finger with the cloth into the vagina and pressing the cloth against all sides. The insertion should be as deep as possible. A superficial examination is not sufficient to be valid."

Should a spot, dot or mark appear on the cloth, the woman is still unclean. If there are any problems, "the cloth should be carefully folded and put into a clean wrapper or envelope and a rabbi must be consulted."

The details proliferate. The cloth must be examined in clear light, not artificial light, in case the colors are not clear. Sometimes people who wear glasses see the spots better without their glasses on. If there is a spot, the woman washes and tries again.

Let's assume that the woman is free of spots or marks. The

rabbis then tell her to put clean white underwear on, and clean white bed linen for seven days more.

What kind of warped mind comes up with ideas like these? I sometimes imagine rooms full of virginal young men in ancient Babylon discussing how long they must wait till she's clean, their sing-song voices rising in excitement as they twist their untidy beards.

Assuming the woman is clean, and has observed the seven clean days, she then goes to the ritual bath or *mikveh.* This idea might have had some rationale behind it in the days when communal baths were the only way for people to wash. But today, when most people have baths in their own homes, the *mikveh* only serves to reinforce the symbolism of the unclean woman washing in order to be acceptable again.

The rabbis have produced the usual detailed series of rules about what may be washed, how the hair must be combed "whilst it is still wet," how eyelashes and brows "must be examined and if necessary washed several times to ensure that no hairs are stuck together," and how "absolutely nothing" must be stuck between the teeth.

Many religions, including Judaism, use immersion in water as a symbol of religious renewal. Converts to Judaism are supposed to be immersed under Orthodox laws. Baptists immerse themselves fully as a sign of their commitment to their faith. Some Baptist churches have a large bath as part of their facilities. And many eastern faiths incorporate bathing in sacred rivers as a ritual of observance.

But only Judaism uses the concept of immersion as a way of making woman clean after her menstrual cycle.

Why Orthodox Women Praise "Niddah" Laws

When Orthodox women have commented on this pattern of behavior, all of them echo the same phrases and words: "It refreshes our marriage,"—"The temporary separation has a stabilizing effect,"—"It revitalizes the marriage bond." I was always surprised that so many of them made the same remarks. Then I read the introduction to the laws. Those phrases describe what women *should* feel about the *niddah*. Like good Jews should, the women dutifully repeat what their rabbis have told them they will feel about these laws, knowing that this is the only right way to behave.

Rabbi Wagschal in the introduction to his translation of the *niddah* laws, writes:

"One need not fear that this periodic separation may be a strain on the marriage. The truth is that temporary separation has a stabilizing influence. It introduces an element of continuous freshness, which revitalizes and strengthens the marriage bond."

That sounds wonderful—but is it true? There have been no objective studies, no scientific comparisons and no long-term analyses of the effects of a law which treats women as unclean because they happen to be menstruating. Certainly, no women's study group has examined the phenomenon objectively.

However, it's important not to miss a paragraph on "Coping with Difficulties":

"It is common to have initial difficulties when attempting to put the laws into practice. There are those who find the calculations complicated. Some are not sure of the timing of the examinations and others find it hard to grasp the practical side."

It seems to me that there are a great many hidden problems in a statement like that. If I were reading a scientific report and found a sentence as significant as that one, I'd want to know exactly what was happening. What are the "initial difficulties"? Why is it hard to "grasp the practical side"? Of course the calculations are complicated: they are ridiculous and quite unworkable, and would drive any woman crazy trying to use them.

One social worker, who sees women from the Orthodox and Hasidic communities, suggested another reason for the acceptance by women of the discriminatory "purity" laws.

"They may be glad to have a reason for refusing sexual advances from their husbands," she said. "Look, these men have little sexual information, and even less experience if they are truly religious. They don't know how to please a woman, how to understand what she wants, how to listen to what she is saying. Sex is simply a right for them, a way of creating more sons. If they follow the laws, they fulfill their sexual duties in the dark, thinking religious thoughts, and never speak to their wives about their feelings or what its like. From what I've seen the experience for most of the women who marry young and in equal ignorance is more like rape than love-making."

Interestingly enough, the idea of learning how to make love to satisfy both partners isn't covered in any of the literature I've found. The emphasis is on the man doing his duty by his wife, so that she won't complain. Modern research shows it takes communication, sharing of feelings and a sensitivity to the other person's viewpoint to bring sexual harmony into a marriage. It takes time and understanding, and a mutual respect. There's little of that in the Orthodox Jewish approach. You don't talk about sex—you think of religious topics. You don't share feelings—you concentrate on improving the embryo. And no man will be sensitive to a woman who is a "lump" to be shaped into a wife, and who's unclean.

It's important to remember that the people who promote the benefits of *niddah* are men, and it is in their interest to keep their wives under control. The introduction is simply propaganda, written by those in power to persuade those without any that the laws are for their own good. It reminds me of the slave-owners who used to assure the slaves that they would never be able to manage in the world outside the plantation without the help of Massa.

The laws themselves look back to a time when women had few rights, no education, and were considered the property of their husbands. By emphasizing the separation of men and women because of the menstrual cycle, the Orthodox and Hasidic authorities hope to keep women subservient and fearful of the contamination, as decreed by ancient beliefs.

Because the community is closed, there's no outside checking on whether the system benefits marital harmony. From what I have read of other family systems which force mandatory separation, it's an unhealthy phenomenon. In studies of Catholic families where birth control was prohibited and sexual relations were limited to the so-called "safe period," there are cases of anger, criticism, and the stress of conforming normal human desire to an arbitrary outside time frame. The sense of performance mandates against a spontaneous sense of affection, knowing that affection must be withheld on some days, but is permitted on others. Mandated matings don't revitalize and refresh; they usually breed self-consciousness and frustration.

It would be interesting as an experiment to observe the differences in family behavior and relationships between an Orthodox pattern and more relaxed rules of sexual behavior.

I'd select 25 couples living by the rules of "niddah" and 25 couples who have chosen a more egalitarian style, and ask them carefully balanced questions. What I'd really like to know is:

—how does a husband feel when he reaches out to embrace his wife, and is brusquely pushed away because she suddenly tells him she is "unclean"?
—how does a wife feel when her husband ostentatiously refuses to sit beside her at dinner and puts a large pitcher of water between them?
—how does a five-year-old child react when his mother is reading him a bedtime story, and he asks his father over to share the moment, but the father refuses to sit by the mother?
—how does a teenage girl feel when her father refuses to sit on the same sofa because he sees, by what she is wearing, that she is menstruating?
—how does a ten-year-old boy feel watching the behavior of mother and father and not understanding what is happening, but aware that no one wants to touch his mother?

Still More Rules

"Family Purity" is often used as a blanket approach to include even more rules to restrict women's freedom of choice.

The favorite word to apply to women is "modesty," and

they are frequently urged to develop that attitude. The rabbis don't hesitate to tell them how to achieve the goal.

Hair: Jewish men are encouraged to grow their sidecurls, develop beards, and look as hairy as possible. Women, on the other hand, are told that hair is naughty.

Rabbi Fuchs, in *A Woman's Guide to Jewish Observance,* notes that, "The Torah forbids a married woman to appear in public with her hair uncovered." In some communities women shave their heads after marriage, and wear a scarf or wig afterwards. Fuchs asserts that, "If a woman's head is shaved the walls of her house will certainly not see the hairs of her head, and she will thereby merit righteous children."

Some authorities forbid wigs, particularly since modern ones are so elegant they look exactly like real hair. Others tell women that they have to cover the wigs with a scarf or other head covering.

In any case, no devout man recites prayers in the presence of a Jewish woman whose hair is uncovered unless he closes his eyes.

Dress: Earlier, I mentioned the laws dictating what women should wear in order to conform to a rabbinic idea of "modesty." These apply to all women, and particularly to married women, even when they are at home.

Bare skin is extremely sinful. There are lengthy rabbinic discourses on whether it is acceptable to allow four inches of skin to be exposed on the arms, or whether that is too reprehensible to be accepted.

Women must cover their necks to the collarbone, their arms to the wrist, their legs completely, and only wear "modest" clothes. If Judaism had invented a long, black wrap like that mandated in Arab cultures, I'm sure the rabbis would be happy to demand that women wore it all the time.

Women cannot wear men's clothes, except for undergarments. Wearing jeans or pants is unacceptable, unless they are worn as protection against cold with a skirt on top.

Rashi, a renowned commentator on the laws, agrees with many of the rules, and asserts: "Bright, red clothing is considered immodest because the clothes are the color of wine and are worn by women to entice."

A friend visiting Jerusalem was about to go into a museum when she noticed a long notice warning women about the necessity for wearing modest clothes and explaining what was acceptable.

"I was insulted," she said. "I was properly dressed by any sensible standards. Frankly, I think there should be dress codes for some of those men in their dirty black clothes with those untidy overgrown beards."

There are also rules about:

A Woman's Voice: A man is forbidden to listen to a woman sing, "and so as not to cause men to transgress this prohibition, women should not sing in their presence."

It's acceptable for the singing children up to the age of eleven to be listened to, but after that it's naughty.

"Girls over the age of eleven who are studying in school or gathered for other purposes should be careful not to sing when they can be heard by people in the street," the rabbis warn sternly.

Now a man can listen to his wife sing, if she's not menstruating and if he is not reciting his prayers. On the other hand, he can sing even if she is praying.

In the Orthodox community where I grew up, a synagogue choir sang during services with the Cantor. One woman with an outstanding voice requested permission to join. She was firmly refused; it was unlawful for women to sing.

And assuming she's not singing, there are plenty of other things she cannot do. These are lumped together under the word *yichud,* which comes from the word "one" in Hebrew, meaning alone. It outlines all the situations where men and women might be alone together, to stop them meeting under any circumstances where a woman might evilly tempt a man with her wicked wiles.

Yichud—Or Being Naughty Alone

Any situation where a man and a woman are alone in any place without a chaperone and are not likely to be disturbed is prohibited by Jewish law. It applies to girls over age twelve,

who may then be alone only with boys under the age of nine.
When a boy is thirteen, he can only be alone with girls under
three.

A man and a woman can be in a room with the door open
"as long as the door remains open and there are people on
the street." And a man and woman may be alone in an un-
locked room "if it is usual for the people in the house to enter
that room without warning."

The thinking behind these kinds of situations shows the
underlying fear of female sexuality. The idea that a man and
a woman could have a business relationship, a friendship, or
a platonic discussion is not conceivable in the rabbinic mind.
The Evil Temptress is always present.

"If a man comes into contact with women in the course of
his profession, he should not be alone with them unless his
wife is present," the book states.

On the other hand a woman may be alone with two or
more men "provided that the men are not lax in sexually-
related matters" suggest the authorities. I wonder how you
check that out when you go into the Post Office or the phar-
macy?

Three women, on the other hand, may be alone only when
there are two or more men. Presumably one man is more
dangerous than two or more.

Travel is a great problem. A man and a woman can travel
in a car through an area as long as there are passersby. Otherwise, you have to have another man in the car, and there
must be minimal traffic, which the rabbis see as "one passing
car every five minutes."

A woman may travel through a populated area in a taxi
driven by a gentile only during the day. And some authorities maintain that these restrictions apply in an elevator.

A woman may not shake a man's hand, even if she is wearing gloves. If she's at a party where it might be expected,
she's advised "to carry a glass or plate of food in her right
hand."

Women may not dance in the presence of men "for by
doing so they cause men to transgress." Mixed dancing with
men and women together is strictly forbidden.

A woman may teach or be a camp counselor for boys under the age of nine, according to one school of thought. On the other hand, another rabbi says the restriction is no longer relevant because women usually teach in places where people are constantly coming and going so that they are not alone.

The essential message of these rules is clear. Women are wicked, sexual beings who must be restrained at all times from tempting men into sinfulness. The rabbis must make sure that women know how dangerous they can be, and keep them securely away from the temptations of independence or autonomy.

It's like living in some maniacal life-size board game where every move involves a complicated sequence of reactions, and where extreme caution is needed to complete the course.

A woman living in this atmosphere is compelled to stay within the fold, withdraw into the security of her family and train her daughters to be fearful, apprehensive and dependent.

It's life in an East European ghetto complete to the last detail. And those within the Orthodox and Hasidic communities are dedicated to making sure that this will be the only acceptable form of Judaism in the future.

And the Rewards?

Rabbinic authorities like to assert that by obeying the laws, devoting themselves to family purity and the observances of family duties and by giving up all independence or individual interests, a woman will be perfectly fulfilled.

Fortunately, such myths are slowly being exploded in the face of reality.

Physicians, psychiatrists and family counsellors now recognize that if a woman focuses her entire being on caring for her family to the exclusion of herself, she will be lost and disoriented when the inevitable occurs: her children grow up and lead their own lives.

Sociologist Pauline Bart recently studied depression in middle-aged women. She examined 533 women between the ages of forty and fifty-nine, who had had no previous hospitalization for mental illness, in Los Angeles County. She took case histories and conducted intensive interviews.

"My suppositions were confirmed," she writes in *The Jewish Woman: New Perspectives.* "Jews have the highest rate of depression. Jewish women are roughly twice as likely to be diagnosed depressed as non-Jewish women.... Overprotection or overinvolvement with children is much more common among Jews than among non-Jews.... All the mothers, when asked what they were most proud of, replied, ' My children.' Occasionally, after this, they mentioned their husbands. None mentioned any accomplishment of their own, except being a good mother."

She found that they demonstrated a classic pre-illness history "of martyrdom with no payoff (and martyrs always expect a payoff at some time) to make up for the years of sacrifice, inability to handle aggressive feelings, rigidity, a need to be useful in order to feel worthwhile, obsessive, compulsive supermother, superhousewife behavior, and generally conventional attitudes."

In the interviews, Bart found that the women felt their children didn't need them, didn't respect them, didn't call or visit them often enough.

Bart notes that the society in which they live provides no guidelines for the time after children are adults: "There is no Bar Mitzvah for menopause.... One thinks of these women as overcommitted to the maternal role, and then, in middle age, suffering the unintended consequences of this commitment."

Because women live longer, and have more years after children are grown, when there is no mothering to be done, the issue of the dedicated mother is becoming more important.

"What I am really talking about here is what happens to women who follow the cultural rules . . . who think there is a payoff for good behavior, who believe in justice, and who therefore suffer depression, a loss of meaning, when they discover that their lives have not turned out the way they expected," Bart says.

"My data shows that it is the women who assume the *tradi-*

tional feminine role—who are housewives, who stay married to their husbands, who are not overtly aggressive, in short who accept the traditional norms—who respond with depression when their children leave," she concludes, and adds:

"The Womens Liberation movement, by pointing out alternate lifestyles, by providing the emotional support necessary for deviating from the ascribed sex roles, and by emphasizing the importance of women actualizing their own selves, and fulfilling their own potentials, can help in the development of personhood."

In another study, Laura B. Wolf, in her M.A. thesis for the University of Houston Graduate School of Social Work, in 1982 examined "The Relationship between Feminism and Depression in Adult Jewish Women."

Her study focussed on more than six hundred women, whom she reached through a Houston Jewish Community Center.

Her results showed that "as adult Jewish women's feminist attitudes increased, so too did their self-esteem. As their self-esteem began to rise, their depressive symptoms began to decrease."

Her conclusion was that "feminism decreases depressive symptoms by increasing self-esteem." And she also felt concern for the stereotypes which men found among Jewish community agencies and suggested changes to help Jewish men adapt to more flexible roles in the family and at work.

9

Fantasy and Reality: Why the Modern World Is Better for Women

The women growing up inside the closed communities of Orthodoxy and Hasidism look at the modern world outside with the same misconceptions that we have when we look into outer space and imagine what life must be like out there.

Fed by stories, myths and the few horrible and frightening events the Jewish media chose to highlight, there's a general conviction that women who venture out of the ghetto face wickedness, cruelty, hazards and misery untold.

They assume that all women are divorced, suffering, abused and desperate. They don't read the magazines that extol the independence of women, or outline the successes women find in business or in sports. They don't see the television documentaries about women achieving success in medicine or in science. And they never meet strong, outspoken women who advocate self-reliance, individual effort and the importance of struggling to achieve personal goals.

I can't imagine that the libraries of Orthodox schools have a subscription to *Ms* magazine, or even publications like *Working Mother,* which reaches women who want to succeed at work and at home. Nor would Betty Friedan's classic on *The Feminine Mystique* be required reading in sociology classes.

Girls and women learn an array of myths about family, about women's abilities and about what life is supposed to be, according to the dictates of the rabbinic tradition.

Let's take a look at some of the teachings which Hasidic and Orthodox leaders present to young people and analyze them in light of sociological studies.

MYTH 1. The sooner you get married, the happier you will be, because it's unhealthy to get married later.

REALITY 1. The marriages which end up in divorce courts most frequently are those between teenagers, or young people who have had limited experience in the world. The statistics show that those who marry later report greater marriage satisfaction, more stable relationships and have a lower divorce rate. It's recognized from many research observations that it takes time for young people to identify what work they choose, how they want to live, and the kind of marriage partner they need.

Other studies show that those with higher education have a higher rate of marriage satisfaction than those with less education.

MYTH 2. Having children makes a marriage perfect.

REALITY 2. There's a well-recognized curve of marital satisfaction. It starts high, in the early days after the wedding and honeymoon. Then it steadily drops after the birth of each child, and in the subsequent years of child-rearing. When the children leave home, the curve slowly rises again. Family counsellors know that the arrival of a baby in the family changes the patterns of behavior within a marriage. The adjustment is difficult, and is repeated with the arrival of each new child. Children's needs shape the framework of a marriage, and often override the preferences of parents.

If there are particular problems with a child, who may be ill or have a handicap, statistics show that the marriage may fall apart. The demands of providing for a family with children can also cause tremendous marital strain.

Other studies show that often couples who choose not to have children rate their marriages as happier than those with children. Having a child is a personal choice for a couple, and there is no evidence that couples with children have a perfect marriage.

MYTH 3. Children need two parents and any child brought up in a situation where a parent is absent is doomed to a life of tragedy.

REALITY 3. In the past, thousands of children were brought up by mothers who were widows and had lost their husbands in cruel wars. Others found themselves alone when husbands deserted them, since divorce was almost unobtainable.

In this generation, when divorce is an accepted way to end a failed marriage, the separation of parents has become more common. At some point in their lives, over half the children under 18 in the United States will spend some time living in a one-parent family. And the children cope. In one study of 289 children in third, sixth and eight grades from two-parent and single parent families, the researchers gave a standard test for self-concept, perception of family structure and family conflict. On every test, there were "no significant differences" among the children, relating to the parental situation. The only children who scored lower on tests were those children in two-parent families where they experienced a great deal of family conflict.

No couple anticipates that their relationship will end in divorce. But it's healthier for two people who no longer want to stay together to separate than to fight constantly in front of the children. Thousands of children have grown up over the centuries in single parent homes very successfully, and will continue to do so.

MYTH 4. Only a woman can care for a home and bring up children because men are incapable of doing so.

REALITY 4. According to a *Time* magazine article, about 800,000 men are single parents, raising children on their own today in the United States. A University of Michigan study of men doing housework between 1965 and 1981 showed that, in the 25 to 44 age group, the amount of time increased by 20 percent.

A woman artist and her teacher husband long ago decided that he would do all the cooking, which he has always done throughout the marriage while they brought up their three daughters. In many, many examples, it's clear that men have the ability to care for children, prepare meals and look after the house. One psychologist noted that it is healthier to divide up duties in the home so that the father feels actively involved, and doesn't become cut off from his children.

MYTH 5. Women are better off without birth control and should never consider abortion.

REALITY 5. Medical experts stress that women should space the births of their children, to give their bodies time to recuperate. They know that having many children exhausts women physically, and they see the consequences.

Abortion has been practiced since Biblical times. It used to be carried out secretly, and in some cases, with poor medical care. Today, women have the choice of deciding whether or not to have a baby, and abortion is an essential part of that issue. It should be a woman's decision as to when and if she chooses to have a baby; she is the one who must go through the pregnancy, the pain of childbirth, and care for the child.

MYTH 6. Never worry about money. Observe all the laws of Judaism, and everything will work out beautifully.

REALITY 6. Family relationships suffer when partners retreat into religious fantasy. Studies show that money problems are a major cause of conflict within marriage. Those families with limited income report more disagreements, difficulties and stress than those where there's an adequate income. In today's economy, it has become more important that both wives and husbands can contribute to the financial support of the family. Today, traditional industries are changing, and often men find themselves unemployed after years of service, so wives work. A family that faces its financial situation realistically is much more likely to survive the strains of marital crises than one that ignores the everyday demands of life.

I've talked to a great many women about their views on Judaism and modern life. I've listened to many stories about how women are coping.

There's always a dividing line between women who choose to stay home and care for their children full time, and women who decide to work in the outside world, and juggle home and career. But that decision can be made in the light of what we know about modern life. We know that if we stay home while our children are little, we may go back to work when they start school. Or we may decide to work part-time while they are growing up. Or we may prefer to devote our time to personal projects we've always wanted to do and focus our energies on home and motherhood for a few years.

Within the extremes of Orthodoxy and Hasidism, the choices are narrowed. I sometimes think of Hanna, one of two sisters, who went to university and studied literature. Somewhere along the way, she became convinced she had to become extremely Orthodox. She began to observe all the minutiae of the laws.

Through a marriage arranger, she met Dov, who had also given up his secular background and college education. He had a job, however, because of his specialized training, as a minor bureaucrat in the government.

They married, and settled in a religious community. Hanna shaved her hair off, and now wears a wig permanently. She has adopted a drab costume of long sleeves, long skirt, thick stockings and heavy shoes. She and Dov had five children, four girls and (T.G.) one boy. They all attend religious schools that emphasize Yiddish, Hebrew studies and Torah.

Dov and Hanna worry constantly that the children might learn something of the outside world, or be tempted to leave the self-imposed ghetto.

"We don't want them to learn English too well, or to watch television or listen to the radio," says Dov. "We want them to stay close to the community."

Hanna is constantly tired. She is always in the house, or preparing food, or caring for the children. She goes to a women's study group occasionally. This year, after the birth of their fifth child, she did not join her family on the two weeks' vacation at an Orthodox summer hotel by the beach. She was too tired.

"When I don't feel well, I go and see our rabbi," she explained. "He's not a doctor, but I tell him what's wrong, and he tells me what to do. Last time he told me to stay home and sip hot tea, and that helped me a little."

There are few books in the house. There are no pictures, except a large photograph of their rabbi. There's no music in the house. There's very little laughter.

They lead a hand-to-mouth existence on Dov's salary. They are giving their children no education or training of any kind to find a job in the world of today. They have in one generation taken their family back into the 19th century, and eliminated all knowledge that might help them survive. They have deliberately accepted ignorance, religious fanaticism and unquestioning devotion to abstruse regulations.

You can find couples like Dov and Hanna in ultra-Orthodox and Hasidic communities in many parts of the country. Some are less devout, some are more so. But all experience the same realities.

Their lives are a constant struggle for survival in a modern world for which they have chosen to avoid any preparation. It's like diving into a swimming pool and deciding to forget how to swim.

Their family experiences are rigidly controlled within a tight, narrow ghetto, and their roles are sharply defined to meet criteria quite alien to today's experiences.

And they propagandize wholeheartedly to those who want to believe that there is something quaint and charming about their experience by emphasizing the celebrations and the warmth of the community. Those exist, but so do the cruelty of discrimination against women, the harshness of the rules, and the bigotry of ultra-Orthodox philosophy.

It isn't poverty that narrows their lives.

I've met people living on low incomes with tolerance, understanding and an appreciation for individual rights.

What freezes their minds is the destructive teachings of the ultra-Orthodox and the Hasidic ways of life.

I'd like to tell you about Anna.

When I first met her, she was in her thirties, married, with two children, and living in a lovely suburban home.

An attractive lively woman, she has an easy laugh and a sense of authority in her manner.

She works as an obstetrician in a major hospital, and with private patients. She has outstanding medical qualifications in a specialized field of obstetrics.

I thought that she had come from a privileged background, encouraged by her parents to become a doctor.

Not so.

She is one of five daughters, born to a poor black couple. Her father was a janitor, and did other odd jobs. Her mother cleaned houses for white families.

But from the very beginning both parents were determined that their children would have something better in their lives.

They wanted to give their children the best they could possibly achieve, opportunities the parents had never been offered.

"My father always said that girls could do just as well as boys, and better, because you can have babies," said Anna. "He was determined that we would all become professional women, and that he would help us to do so. He told us not to get married early, as he had done, and not to have children until we were thirty. And he warned us not to get involved with a boy until we could earn our own money and be independent."

She and her sisters were encouraged to work hard at school, to do their homework, to study regularly.

"My mother would never let us help in the kitchen," remembers Anna. "If we stopped studying and came down, she would make us scrub the floor and then say, if you like doing that you can do it for the rest of your life. If you study, you won't have to do the cleaning."

When one daughter expressed interest in music, their father bought her a trombone. Then, as the other girls grew up, he formed them into a band to play in public. They had music lessons and practiced regularly. But he always told them that the music would not be their lives.

Despite the discrimination of the times, their father sent all five girls to college. Two of them went on to become doctors, one became a dentist and one a teacher. The eldest trained as an executive secretary "because she couldn't stand the sight of blood."

Today, all the sisters are independent women, four of them married with children. They are bringing up their own children with the same dedication to the high ideals of their father. And they are preparing a new generation to take their place in the modern world.

"I don't know how he knew so much then," Anna says, "but everything he told us came true. He always encouraged us all to do the very best we could, and we'd succeed."

Sometimes I think of Hanna, struggling in the dingy apartment with five children, accepting without question the oppressive regime of the rules of ultra-Orthodox Judaism; and Anna, sitting in her office at the hospital sharing her knowledge and expertise with women who come to see her, and with students eager to learn how they too can help others.

It's as if one woman has turned her back on the future, and rejected life, while the other has struggled for her advantages and now shares them with those who need her help.

Where Extremism Is Leading

Hasidim and ultra-Orthodox Jews have much in common with the views and attitudes of the repressive regime of the extremist Muslims. Just like the present rule in Iran, Jewish zealots would relish seeing all women shackled to strictly conformist clothing. They would be delighted if women received minimal education. And they would be perfectly happy if their lives revolved round children, home and kitchen.

These attitudes might have been a little extreme even in the past. Today, they are prehistoric. The bigotry is laughable in this present flowering of change in women's lives. And the effrontery of ignoring the benefits must not go unchallenged.

Liberal, Reform and other thinking Jews have an obligation to speak out clearly against the distortion of basic Jewish teachings. The broad-based learning of Judaism has many, many laws and even more interpretations.

There's a story about a cynical man who asked a famous rabbi to tell him about Judaism in a few minutes, while he stood on one leg. The rabbi calmly replied:

"Do unto others only as you would have them do unto you. That is the whole teaching of Judaism," showing the basic simplicity of its deepest beliefs.

There are Jewish laws about tolerance, about accepting the stranger in the community as a Jewish equal if he behaves in an honorable fashion, of learning in as many areas as possible, and of honoring the laws of the country in which you are living.

There are liberal rabbis who argue conclusively that Jewish law has always been in favor of birth control and accepts abortion. There are interpretations of laws which accept the idea that any law may be broken if there is a danger to life. There are laws which urge Jews to find secular jobs within the community and not dedicate themselves solely to studying the Bible and the Talmud. But the Orthodox take a rigid male-oriented interpretation and ignore other alternatives.

It's difficult to speak out. The immediate reaction is a passionate cry of "anti-Semite!" For any Jew to criticize the behavior of other groups is to walk into a battlefield littered with landmines. Like many in extremist positions, the ultra-Orthodox don't argue rationally or discuss issues. They simply attack with emotion. They assert that anyone who sees Hasidism or ultra-Orthodoxy as destructive and unhealthy is anti-Semitic. They insult the religious beliefs of any Jew who offers criticisms of their discrimination against women. And they have no hesitation in harassing and attacking those with whom they disagree, or who present more tolerant viewpoints of interpretations of Jewish law.

When the mayor of Jerusalem, Teddy Kollek, came to New York on an official visit, thousands of black-garbed Hasidim paraded outside his hotel protesting his visit, because they objected to decisions he had made about behavior in Jerusalem.

It's become a common sight in New York to see hordes of Hasidim herded like sheep protesting deviations from what they see as the proper path.

But the tone of the protests is changing. What was merely religious zeal is becoming fanatic. Several recent incidents typify the trend.

- In Israel, in 1986, ultra-Orthodox groups destroyed more than 100 public bus shelters. Why? They objected to an advertising poster showing a woman with more than the acceptable amount of bare skin showing. There are many ways of objecting to a poster. Destroying bus shelters is an exaggerated response, the reaction of unbridled hooligans unable to behave rationally. The pictures did no harm to anyone. There were no complaints. There was no public criticism. But taking the law into their own hands, the ultra-religious showed that they felt their beliefs overrode the common standards, and the comfort of the hundreds of Israelis who used the bus shelters. The orthodox asserted that it was insulting to women to allow such portrayals to be shown. No women's group as far as I can ascertain asked them to go and tear down bus shelters in defense of feminine modesty.

These attitudes toward women are carried to ludicrous extremes. In a recent case in Orange County, in the Kiryas Joel community, about sixty miles outside of Manhattan, a group of rabbis refused to allow the little boys who attend the United Talmudic Academy to ride school buses driven by

women. The buses are provided by the Monroe-Woodbury
School district, even though the school is not a public one.

I can't help wondering what they thought might happen to
a busful of little boys in a bus driven by a woman. Did they
imagine the sight of the back of the driver's head would im-
pel the embryo Hasidim to an orgy of sexuality? Were they
frightened that the driver, whom they see as the usual evil
temptress, would stop the bus and indulge in unimaginable
wickedness with the innocent youngsters? Or were they
worried that the idea of a woman driving a bus might im-
plant the idea that women were capable and responsible and
not lightheaded and foolish, as they had been told?

One of the women drivers, Brenda Mercurio, stated:

"On the coach buses used to transport Hasidim to New
York City, separation of the sexes is accomplished by a curtain down the middle. . . . The bus drivers offered to drive
with a curtain separating them from the male students. This
offer was not accepted."

The Hasidim demand male bus drivers. The women drivers accuse them of discrimination. The issue is now in the
courts.

The same kind of hysterical reaction occurred in a Reform
synagogue, during the celebration of the week-long religious
festival of Tabernacles. On the last evening, there is rejoicing
at the completion of the annual reading of the five books of
Moses, the Torah, and the day is called "Simhat Torah."

- During the evening service celebrating the festival, when
  men, women and children were rejoicing together in the
  Reform synagogue, an Orthodox rabbi burst in, with some
  followers. He shouted angrily, "This place is a whore-
  house!" and protested at the men and women dancing together. Then he tried to steal the scrolls of the law and take
  them outside. Fortunately, the group surrounded the men
  in a circle, and rescued the scrolls.

This behavior is a sad reflection on the interpretation of
Judaism, and its beliefs. And the attitudes are hardening in
other areas.

- Since 1916, during the First World War, there's been a
commission of representatives from Orthodox, Conservative and Reform communities to approve the appointment of rabbis to serve as chaplains in the armed forces.
In 1986, the name of a young woman came forward for
approval. A trained Reform rabbi, she was to be appointed as a Navy chaplain. The Orthodox rabbis objected. "Orthodox Judaism cannot accept women rabbis,"
said a representative. The majority supported the decision. The Orthodox group then withdrew from the commission.

The exodus was another sign of their growing retreat
from reality in the face of changes in women's lives. They
simply refused to recognize the rights of any woman to become a religious leader. Even though the woman was not Orthodox, they refused to recognize her capabilities or
qualifications.

Later, official arguments explained that Orthodox beliefs
allow women to accept family obligations, but they cannot
make decisions on conversion, marriage or divorce. The il-
logical reasoning of this argument is clear. If conversion or
marriage or divorce are not family obligations, what are?
The many women Reform rabbis have learned that their
perspective on family obligations help them serve their
communities in ways that men may not be able to.

The Orthodox withdrawal from the commission reflected
their lack of concern with the legalities of other bodies of authority. The commission, in existence for sixty years,
reflected the majority view of the Jewish community. In a democracy, one of the essential concepts is that we abide by majority decisions. Even when the candidate we want is not
elected, we accept the vote and continue to obey the laws under the person elected by the majority.

Orthodoxy fosters anarchy. If the decisions are not what
the Orthodox like, they'll just pretend they didn't happen.
Like a petulant child who suddenly finds that what he wants
is no longer permitted, the Orthodox man disdains the deci-

sions of most Jews, and demands adherence to his own perverse view of women.

Orthodox and Hasidic men seem to be asserting that, no matter what the ruling, their views will prevail in the land. To whom are they answerable? How can a woman expect a fair hearing in such an atmosphere? What kind of rule of law will develop under such repression?

There's no pretense of democracy within such communities. Among Hasidics, the rabbi-leader of the group is appointed by the rabbi-leader in power. Like a king, he is revered. There's no recourse of any kind for criticism, complaints or change. There's no acceptance of the concept one-person-one-vote which is the foundation of the United States Constitution.

At the frequent men-only meetings where the rabbi-leader addresses his followers in Yiddish, he spouts platitudes and out-dated teachings which they accept wholeheartedly. Afterwards, the men scramble to eat a crumb from the rabbi-leader's plate, fighting over the leftovers, struggling forward to touch his coat, or his hand.

The women either are hidden behind a screen or not present at all.

It's the same fanatic obsession that you find in the televised hokum of the Christian charismatic meetings or the ecstasies of revivalist gatherings. Reason, common sense and rational thinking are never present.

Young girls and women within Orthodoxy and Hasidism are persuaded to believe superstitions and fantasies about their abilities and their behavior, based on long out-dated religious attitudes.

In Israel, a court case typifies the clash that may be inevitable.

Every Jewish town in Israel has a city council to handle municipal administration. There is also a state financed religious council, to sponsor religious programs, pay the rabbi's salary, and oversee the Jewish cemetery, marriage office and ritual baths. Usually, only men serve on the religious council.

Three years ago, an Orthodox woman, Leah Shakdiel, a

schoolteacher, was elected to the city council on the Labor Party ticket, in a small town called Yeroham.

The city council chooses four of the nine people on Yeroham's religious council, and the Ministry of Religious Affairs chooses four. The local rabbis appoint the rest. Due to conflicts in the coalition nominations, Ms. Shakdiel was left with the deciding vote. She forced the city council to nominate her for the religious council, in February 1985.

A Ministry official then wrote to her: "I can already tell you it is not within the realm of the possible. In the religious council there are no woman councilors. Only men serve."

In a newspaper interview in *The New York Times*, Ms. Shakdiel said:

"Actually he wrote, 'only men *can* serve on it' but he erased that because he realized that the law does not say such a thing."

Some rabbis object to the idea of sitting on a council with a woman. But Ms. Shakdiel said firmly:

"I don't doubt their sincerity when they say that some rabbis are embarrassed to sit with women. I think some of them are, and its a pity we have such a generation of rabbis. But I would say, nowhere does the law say that only rabbis have to sit on the religious councils. If they have a hard time sitting with me O.K., don't be there."

At present, the Ministry of Religious Affairs refuses to recognize Ms. Shakdiel's nomination, and is preventing Yeroham's religious council from meeting. According to a newspaper report, the Knesset has scheduled a full debate on the dispute, which may only be resolved in Israel's Supreme Court.

The crisis reflects the crux of the conflict between ancient religious views on women and the realities of modern life, where women take an active political role.

10

Getting Out: How I Escaped to Save My Sanity and Survive

The first time I rode in a car on the Sabbath I was sixteen years old. The moment is as clear in my mind as it was when I did it, over thirty years ago. It's more vivid than my first kiss.

Orthodoxy has established priorities for judging Good Observant Jews from Bad Deviant Jews. For some reason, riding on the Sabbath is a major difference. Kissing is not considered naughty. Even murder isn't given the same intense discussion as whether or not someone rides on the Sabbath.

To suggest there's nothing wrong with driving a car to the synagogue is to call into question ethical behavior, moral standards, devotion to the faith and eternal damnation in Hell.

A friend told me a story of the time her mother was in the hospital and an Orthodox man from the synagogue visited her.

"He arrived one Sabbath afternoon, and made a big point of emphasizing how he had walked over," she said. "My mother, who was in pain, tried hard to be polite and make conversation. But there was only one thing he wanted to discuss: whether or not he had broken the Sabbath laws by taking the elevator to her room. When another friend arrived, he monopolized the entire visiting time discussing the details of the problem, and bringing in all kinds of other examples."

I understand that mindset. I can remember when I believed riding on the Sabbath was equal to lying to your parents. No matter how many Good Deeds you performed it was diabolical to ride on the Sabbath.

The first break came when I decided it was a foolish law. I expressed this to my friends. One of them said, "Why do you bother to keep it then?"

"Because of my parents," I replied.

"Well, when are you going to do what you want to do?" he asked.

That weekend, he invited me to a party. He said he would come and pick me up in his car well before the Sabbath had ended on that long summer day.

I agreed, but suggested he park his car a few blocks away.

He arrived at the house. I said goodbye to my parents, and we walked to his car.

He opened the door and I got in.

He walked round to his side of the car and got in.

He started the car.

I sat there, holding my breath, terrified, waiting for the long streak of forked lightning that would flash through the windshield and strike me dead on the spot.

Nothing happened.

Nothing at all.

The car started, we drove off and we had a great time at the party.

For me, it proved what I firmly believed. The Lord, wherever He or She might be, was not in the least interested in whether people rode on the Sabbath. It was unimportant in the great scheme of things that occurred in the world.

After that I deliberately but discreetly travelled to other parts of town on the Sabbath, taking buses, trains or cars, but hoping I wouldn't meet my parents' friends.

My parents encouraged me to go out to parties, to social events, and to meet people. The essence of a young girl's life in a modern Orthodox community is like that of a debutante.

The idea is that the sooner a young Jewish girl meets a Nice Jewish Boy, the sooner she will become engaged, get married and settle down. The idea of loose, unattached and independent women (and men) is anathema to Jewish parents. Once you have your diamond on your left hand finger, you're set. Your parents can heave a sigh of relief, your friends can harbor jealousy and your future is planned to the last detail.

One young woman who decided, after several months of her engagement, that she didn't want to go through with the marriage was shocked by her family's reaction.

"My mother kept urging me to marry him and work things out afterwards," she said. "She told me I could get a divorce but at least I should get married. It was as if she couldn't bear the responsibility of seeing me single and it was better to be married to anyone than stay alone. I couldn't believe it."

It's an approach totally out of touch with the realities of today's world.

From the age of fourteen or fifteen, I went to social events at the synagogue, to attend social clubs, to meet people, to smile and flirt with all available young men.

I had party dresses, elegant shoes and new clothes for every occasion. And I had my unruly hair combed and backcombed and curled and set frequently.

I didn't hold out particularly high hopes for my immediate marriage. I was part of a group of friends, and one or two actually went out together. But I hadn't noticed young men falling over themselves with excitement when I walked into a room, as they often did when the exuberant buxom Renee did. Nor did they crowd around my chair to chat with me as they seemed to do with quiet dark-haired Ruth. And they didn't call me up on the phone to walk over to the synagogue with them as they did with vivacious Leslie.

On the other hand, I didn't find any of the young men of special interest in any way. They were pleasant, and friendly. But they seemed to accept the rules and regulations to which

I objected. They didn't seem to see anything wrong with the law relating to women. They seemed perfectly happy to go on as their fathers and grandfathers had done.

I trotted along to charity dances, to community celebrations and to friends' birthday parties.

I was always aware of how I wasn't going to make it. My mother's eagle eye would run over my dress, my shoes and my hair and make some critical comment which deflated any optimism I might have harbored. She herself loved the challenge of dressing elegantly, looking fashionable. She made it quite clear that I would never measure up to her standards as the "perfect daughter."

"You can't wear that jacket with that dress," she would say, as I came down the stairs.

"But I don't have anything else," I would say.

"Go and put on the other dress, the one with the matching jacket," she would assert. So I would change. Or I would argue, depending on my mood.

But whatever I did, she would never compliment me. It was as if saying kind things might have a disastrous effect on me. She might say, "That's better" or "You look tidy at least." Then I would be off to an agonizing evening at a huge Bar Mitzva of friends of theirs, or a fund-raising charity dance for Israel, or a dance at the synagogue hall. I'd stand at the side of the room, perhaps with two or three girlfriends, giggling and talking and trying to pretend we weren't trying to attract the attention of the boys, who were equally self-conscious. The relationships were forced and uncomfortable. We had no reason to meet except to pair off like our parents. And we felt we had failed if no one asked us to dance.

It's one of the ironies of my rejection of Orthodoxy that I came remarkably close to fulfilling all the right expectations.

At one of the more lavish charity events, a young man of 21, studying to be a lawyer, invited me to dance. He seemed much older than I. There's quite a gulf between a schoolgirl of sixteen and a college graduate of 21. I was immensely flattered, particularly since he was charming and articulate, and thought I was wonderful.

He took my phone number at the end of the evening and called me the next day. To my surprise, my parents didn't object at all when I went out with him on my own for the evening. The relationship developed into a romantic summer love affair, full of excitement and discovery. My friends were immensely impressed, my social life flourished and I was ecstatically happy.

Throughout this time, my parents never discussed what was going on. They continued to make comments about my marrying soon, and I suppose looking back that they thought their prayers has been answered. I would marry this pleasant law student, and their worries would be over.

But things did not work out as planned. There were two problems. When September came around, I said I could only go out at weekends. The pressure of schoolwork and college preparation were something I had decided to take seriously. When I told him, he was surprised. He had no such demands and wanted to go out and enjoy himself. And the other problem was that other young men started to call and ask me out. And I thought that might be fun too.

It was an interesting dichotomy. If I'd been truly devoted to the Orthodox ideal, I might have seen my first boyfriend as the perfect solution. We could have continued to go out, got engaged and I might have been married at seventeen.

But whatever had driven me to examine the reality of Orthodox life also encouraged me to go on with my studies, to make friends with other young men, and to explore and develop my interests. Hardly the path to marriage.

The end was inevitable. One evening, after an unsatisfactory stroll round a local park, we had a short discussion. He told me that I wasn't ready to have a serious relationship, and that he wanted to go out with other girls who weren't studying all week. I was devastated. I didn't know what to say. This had never been part of my wildest imaginings. I wanted him to be around in my life; I just wanted him to wait for a while until I tried some of the wonderful things I wanted to do on my own.

My parents were equally shattered. My mother said sharply, "You shouldn't have wasted your time on your school work."

But she and my father sympathized with the pain of a broken heart. He never called again. A few years later when I was working as a journalist, I met him at a friend's wedding. I couldn't believe that this rather plump, awkward young man might have been my husband. We talked cheerfully, and I left with an overwhelming sense of relief.

The Double Standard

When I grew up, most girls accepted the excruciating double standard of sexual attitudes. A girl must be a virgin, but a man was allowed to have "experience." Logically, you have to wonder where he found this experience, but I wasn't aware enough to ask questions like that.

I believed absolutely that you only slept with (which, by the way, I took quite literally) the man you married. I had the unshakable conviction of the innocent that love was perfect, lasted for ever and virginity was the only state until marriage, after which it would be eternal physical and emotional bliss.

I was also absolutely ignorant about sexual intercourse, about what actually took place, how women conceived, how babies were born or what you might do to stop getting pregnant.

My parents had no interest in educating me on any of these topics. No one told them, so why should they tell me?

Young men were supposed to be aggressive, macho and sexually adept. The gossip on the grapevine knew who went with whom, and what they did. Certainly Nice Jewish Boys did not hesitate when left alone with Nice Jewish girls. Hormones are not trained in Orthodox niceties. But no one ever admitted what was happening.

I never told my parents my experiences with my first boyfriend, and the innocent affection which amazed me. They never mentioned the possibility of any physical relationship between us. It was a kind of silent approval, without comment.

It was made clear that we couldn't discuss this, though there might be oblique references, such as, "You sat out in the car late last night," along the way.

Today, I understand only too well how vulnerable I was—and how helpless.

It's unspeakably irresponsible for parents to allow their daughters to go out alone with young men without telling them about intercourse, birth control and what to expect. I'm not recommending a lecture on the doorstep as she goes out the door. But in the years beforehand, it's vital that young girls understand what is happening, what can happen and how to say no if they don't want it to happen.

Young women have to understand sexual behavior, and be aware of what is going on before it's too late. Love and passion are overwhelming at any point. But love and passion in total ignorance can be disastrous.

It's the Biblical approach to life, set down by men, which is sadly out of touch with the reality of today. You can lock up your daughters, and send them out pure and ignorant on an arranged marriage, to serve as a man's property for their life together. Or you are bound to give your daughters information, discussion, answers and support to understand the relationships with men.

Today's world is a difficult one for young women in new and unexpected ways. Parents have an obligation to provide as much help as they possibly can along the way.

I'm sure these experiences are still true today for young women growing up with Orthodox or Hasidic groups. And it's true for many other young women in other communities of other religions and other backgrounds.

For a variety of reasons, the knowledge that's available today about sexuality and its consequences is sometimes suppressed. The very people who should have access to the best information are often left the most ignorant of the facts.

I can't pretend to understand the complicated reasons that lie behind every community's decisions to hide sexual realities from its young women and men. I speak only from my own experience. In the Orthodox belief, the more repressed young women are and the less freedom they have, the better it is for everyone. I never believed that. It's like telling starving people that they are better off eating dry bread and water instead of the elegant meals which are available, because they wouldn't like them, and they aren't mature enough to cope.

I don't believe it. Young girls (and young boys too) are quite capable of understanding the truth about their bodies and their emotions, if it's presented in a healthy, positive framework. It's an insult to their sensitivity, intelligence and abilities to deprive them of knowledge that will help them make wise decisions.

The consequences were always visible in the past, though covered up for the sake of propriety. Young women gave birth to babies and then gave them up for adoption. Adoption societies and official homes had many unwanted babies of Nice Girls who found out too late what passion could lead to. The rates of infanticide were high too, where babies were left outside to die, or were simply abandoned by over-wrought mothers. Or young girls would go away for several months to visit relatives and then return as if nothing had happened, to cover up an unwanted pregnancy.

Even today, there are stories like that of the pregnant fifteen-year-old who didn't dare tell her parents, and then committed suicide by lying down on railway tracks. Or the teenager who believes she's not pregnant until the baby is suddenly born, because she doesn't understand what is happening.

And "shotgun marriages" still occur, though not as often as in the past. That's when a young man made a young girl pregnant, and, under the threat of the shotgun of her out-raged father, married her. Many of these marriages were un-happy, forcing together two young people with little in common but their moment of sexual expression. One woman with two children described to me how her parents insisted she marry the sailor she had met at a dance when she was just eighteen, and by whom she became pregnant.

"He didn't want to marry me, and I only thought that I had to because of the baby," she said. "He went back to sea. I saw him once more two years later. He came to see me for a weekend, and that's when I got pregnant again. I've never had another boyfriend. I don't hear from my husband at all. I don't know where he is."

I met her at an evening class in Spanish, where she was trying to fulfill the requirements for her high school diploma. She lived in a small apartment, worked as a waitress and coped with her two children, who were just starting school.

"My parents never wanted to help," she said. "They said that it was my fault. But I didn't know anything. I had no idea I would get pregnant because of what happened that evening. I didn't understand what was going on, and no one had ever told me anything about it."

It's a story which has been repeated in endless variations throughout history. But today, there are unique opportunities for women to learn about the realities before the moment of no return.

Groups like the Hasidim and ultra-Orthodox are faced with a dilemma. In the past, girls and women were isolated and shut away. In a description of an Arab village wedding, Elizabeth Warnock Fernea in *Guests of the Sheik* describes how the bride, dressed up and ornamented with gold and make-up, sits waiting all day until her groom comes to claim her. Not until after the wedding celebration will the groom come to her room to rape her. The groom's mother and the bride's mother then show the blood-stained sheet, proof that the girl's hymen had been ruptured and that she was an untouched virgin.

With total isolation and complete subservience, men can keep control of the lives of women.

However, in our century women of all backgrounds have found freedom and independence as never before. Once young girls have been educated, and shown that they can lead lives of their own, how can they be kept within the narrow fold of Orthodoxy? And if they are given some modicum of freedom in their relationships with men, then it is essential to give them the knowledge of birth control, an understanding of sexuality and the opportunity to make their own decisions.

The extremist religious groups are caught. They understand the need to show some understanding of the far-reaching changes in women's lives. But at the same time, they don't want to admit how far those changes will lead. They are reluctant to give up their power of control, or to share leadership with women. So they persist in demanding virginity and obedience. The hypocrisy is even more dangerous for young girls.

Breaking Free

To escape from Orthodoxy you have to change your pattern of eating, your pattern of working, your pattern of thinking, and your pattern of relating to men and women. Sometimes I wish I could take the memory cells of knowledge and information about Orthodox behavior which I accumulated during my years of indoctrination and hand them over to someone else who's interested in the experience.

The calendar is entirely focused on the Jewish Holy Days. The Jewish New Year comes in autumn, followed by the Day of Atonement, the most solemn day of the year when you are supposed to fast and pray for inclusion in next year's book of life. Once you have been exposed to that experience year after year, it's hard to wipe out the automatic sense of preparation for the High Holy Days as they're sometimes called. As the summer ends, and the cool nights arrive, there's an internal clock which expects the traditional celebrations and interruption of routine.

There's the awareness of Jewish restaurants and Jewish stores, because you have learned to look out for such places as "acceptable" to eat in. You spot "kosher" butchers and produce with "Kosher for Passover" labels. You notice people dressed up and walking to the synagogue and realize that it's the festival of Shavuot, or Weeks, which comes in the summer as one of the three Harvest Festivals. Or you notice the erection of leaf-covered huts in backyards, which signifies the celebration of Succoth, or Tabernacles, commemorating the time the Jews lived in simple tents in the wilderness.

You know the rules about how women are supposed to behave. You may reject them; you may refuse to honor them. But you have been taught that women are unclean and that they cannot touch the holy scrolls of the Law. The indoctrination is so deep that it is impossible to eradicate.

One woman who left the Orthodox community and joined a liberal synagogue where women are called to the reading of the Law and fully participate in services admitted:

"This year I was invited to carry a Torah on Simhat Torah [the Rejoicing of the Law]. However, I did not feel worthy of the honor and refused. Here my Orthodox upbringing lingers. . . . But even though I myself have no desire to lead a congregation, despite my ancestry, I am delighted that other women have the opportunity to do so."

I look at the photo in a book showing a group of young boys and girls with their teacher, examining an unrolled scroll of the Torah, and I marvel that the girls are present.

How wonderful that they are allowed to be treated just like boys! Who was brave enough to stand up and break the barrier of discrimination for them?

I'm also aware that I will always have the strange ability to understand the perspective of the ultra-Orthodox viewpoint. I can remember clearly the unquestioned disdain for all non-Jews that was an accepted attitude of the community. I know the ignorance, the lack of information and absence of knowledge about life outside the closed doors of the community. I understand that it is absolutely impossible to hope for tolerance or compassion or sympathy from the truly devoutly Orthodox when faced with someone who disagrees.

The closest analogy to leaving Orthodox Judaism I've found are the descriptions of people who have left extremist cults or given up the Catholic priesthood. There are now groups to help people adjust to the real world outside after years of living inside such a protective environment. Self-help groups like Fundamentalists Anonymous teach participants to take responsibility for their actions, and to rid themselves of the harmful beliefs they absorbed during their time inside the cults.

There's a sense of leaving a world behind, of closing a door through which no re-entry is permitted. Those inside are convinced that they are right, and anyone who leaves is a traitor or defector from the truth.

In some cases, it's the beliefs which people have to learn to discard. With Orthodoxy and Hasidism, it's the compulsions as well. Once you leave, you have to decide that you will no longer observe the laws of eating meat and milk. You have to realize that you will not observe the details of Sabbath observance. And you recognize that you cannot abide by the laws of modesty and subservience essential for womanly behavior.

There are Orthodox Jews who don't keep all those laws. They learn to behave as discreetly as possible, even though they don't observe the details. As long as they continue to profess adherence to the ideal, they're accepted.

But it's not acceptable for anyone to publicly criticize the traditional attitudes and observances.

The reasons for this I absorbed in my childhood. Somehow, those who lived by the standards of Orthodoxy were better people, more honorable Jews, kinder parents, stronger morally and unquestionably closer to what God originally wanted in the Bible.

There was no objective analysis of this assumption. Everyone *knew* that we were the Chosen, and those outside were the Lost.

Despite the fact that rumors and gossip showed that men were unfaithful to their wives, that sometimes people were dishonest, that on occasion people worked on the Sabbath, and that not everyone was as kind and generous and thoughtful as was expected, no one questioned the fundamental conviction of superiority.

When impossible and unrealistic standards of behavior are forced on human beings, honesty and truth fly out of the window. People hide what they are doing. They lie about their actions. They ignore their feelings to preserve the outward signs of harmony. They struggle to conform to the impossible ideals of perfection. Hypocrisy is the only means of survival.

My parents never understood my criticisms. As long as I didn't embarrass them publicly, they were prepared to ignore my lapses. If I took a bus on the Sabbath, I knew that I had to walk two stops away so no one saw me.

If, when I began working, I decided not to come home

early in time for Friday night's Sabbath, I had to sneak into the house quietly and try not to let the neighbors notice.

And when one friend arrived in a car on the Sabbath, he was politely requested to park it round the corner so no one would know whose it was. The idea that we might have friends who were less Orthodox than the accepted norm was too embarrassing to contemplate.

You might imagine that an extremist Orthodox or Hasidic parent, faced with a child who won't accept the rigid rules of behavior, observance and belief would encourage the deviant to join a less fervent group of Jews, like the Conservative or Reform Jewish communities. At least it's Judaism, they might think.

That's like suggesting that if you don't make the American Olympic swim team you might swim for the Russians.

The inter-group rivalry among different brands of Judaism is most vicious, particularly among the ultra-Orthodox and Hasidic groups who specialize in wholesale intolerance. For an Orthodox person to join a Reform community is akin to disaster. It's Orthodoxy, or Hasidism, or Nothing.

For a time, I worked at a settlement house in a poor part of London, helping with the children's playgroups in the afternoons. I met a young Reform rabbi there.

I mentioned him casually to my parents one Friday evening, because of a comment he had made. Both my parents winced when they realized he was a Reform Jew.

Later my mother urged me to give up the friendship.

"Why?" I said. "We see each other at the Settlement House, we talk about what we're doing, and that's about it."

She sighed. "Who knows where these things will lead?" she said. "You want to stop it right away, before anything happens. And you know, you're breaking your father's heart by going out with a Reform Jew."

Her last two words made him sound like an incipient Nazi storm trooper.

The relationship never led in any of the dire directions my mother predicted. He went off to travel, and that was the end of it.

But it was attitudes like this that made me understand there was no comfortable acceptance of diversity in my experience of Judaism. I publicly behaved like a Good Orthodox Jew, or I was Out.

I longed to Get Out.

But the practicalities loomed large. How could I earn money and support myself? Where could I live? What could I do to survive?

The Shabbas Goy

My outspoken rebelliousness made me the ideal person to become the "Shabbas Goy" in the family. Every family needs one, because there are so many things forbidden on the Sabbath. For example, you cannot turn the lights on or off, on the reasoning that you are causing work for the electricity, and work is forbidden on the Sabbath. So there are a variety of solutions.

We had a timer to turn the light off on Friday evening at 11 p.m. and on again the following afternoon. Once, when a girlfriend was staying over the weekend, she almost tripped down the stairs trying to find the bathroom in the middle of the night. None of the lights would turn on before the appointed time.

I expressed myself clearly. "It's crazy not to turn on the lights, because electricity runs no matter what," I said. "I will turn them on and off."

Now, the law says you cannot actually ask another Jew to break the rules for you. But if she does it without asking, you don't criticize. So no one could actually say, "Would you turn out the living room lights?" But if I did it, and they knew that I did, it was acceptable as long as they didn't ask.

My brother, who later become ultra-Orthodox too, knew the rules. My parents often went to bed before us, and we would sit reading downstairs. When he had gone to bed, my task was to turn off the lights, and then go to his bedroom and turn out his bedroom light. He would never ask me to do it, nor thank me afterwards. But if I didn't, it stayed on all night.

I'd become the "Shabbas Goy" or Sabbath Non-Jew who does all the things Jews won't do in order to keep the Sabbath.

There's an elderly lady who lives on the 15th floor of a New York hotel. At ten o'clock on Saturday mornings she stands by the elevator, but she won't ring the bell. She has to wait until someone else on her floor comes along, or the cleaning man who knows she needs help shows up. Then the bell is pushed, and she takes the elevator to the lobby and walks to the synagogue.

That's what she needs a "Shabbas Goy" for.

You can have a hot meal or a cup of tea if the "Shabbas Goy" willingly makes it. You can have things brought to the house in a car. You can have a fire lit in the grate. You can have the dishes cleared up.

All of these roles I willingly filled. It didn't bother me at all. It confirmed my conviction that the rules were foolish since there were so many subterfuges to get around them.

As I turned sixteen and expressed my criticisms and my concerns about Orthodox patterns of behavior, there was little outward change visible. I continued to be a part of the same Orthodox community. I continued to behave as I was expected to behave. And while my faith evaporated as rapidly as a muddy puddle dries up in the sunshine, there were no outward signs that anything was wrong.

Over the next five years, very slowly but quite deliberately, I forced myself to break away and find my own path.

One Friday evening there was an unexpected drama. I was now almost as tall as my father. Before the meal on Friday evening, when the two candles and the loaves of bread stand on the table with the wine and the salt, the father places his hands on his children's head and blesses them. For the boys, he asks that they grow up like their ancient forefathers. For the girls, that they grow up like Sarah and Rebecca, the Biblical mothers. I had come to the conclusion that I no longer wished to grow up like Sarah and Rebecca.

The image of the religious tradition is usually described as the father holding his hands over two young children with their heads bent. There's no provision for the moment when they are taller than he is.

When the moment came to stand up and receive the usual blessing, I said:

"I don't want a child's blessing any more. I'm not a child."

My father looked startled. My mother said quickly, "Don't be silly. Do what you're supposed to do." My brother said nothing, but stared in amazement.

"I don't want to be blessed. I'm not a little child," I said, keeping my voice calm, and staying in my seat. There was silence. Then my father blessed my brother. There was absolutely no further discussion of the issue. I didn't mention it again. I simply avoided the moment of blessing. My parents never brought the topic up. It was ignored—the safest way to deal with any problem, according to their reasoning.

The fact that I went to the synagogue less and less frequently on the Sabbath was an occasional source of discussion. But since teenagers hate getting up early, and many of my friends did not attend regularly, this too became accepted. On Jewish Holy Days, it was imperative to attend, and so I acquiesced.

But the words of the services and the pattern of the prayers became ludicrous. Why was there an impassioned plea to return to Israel and no one even dreamt of moving there? Why was there so much repetition of prayer after prayer so services dragged on for hours? What was so spiritual about listening to quavery-voiced men read from the Torah as if women could not do it equally as well? Why didn't the community honor thirteen-year-old girls like they did boys? I began to use the time in synagogue for personal reflection, for thinking about issues which concerned me and I ignored the rote prayers.

I was leading an intensely confusing double life. At school the emphasis was on college preparation and demanding academic study. We had a great deal of homework, reading and class preparation. The message was clear; girls must stretch their minds and move out into the world.

At home, my parents' major concern was that I marry soon. At one point my mother suggested I leave school at sixteen, which was an educational option, and take a secretarial course.

"You don't need to go on with your education if you are going to get married," she said firmly. "What's the point of all this additional school?"

"I want to go on to college if I can," I said, not being too sure why, but positive it was more interesting than marriage. "And I want to travel and find a job which interests me and that I want to do."

My mother sniffed. "Waste of time and money!" she said firmly. "Girls don't need any of that. You can just leave now and you know quite enough."

"I'd like to stay on at school until I'm eighteen," I said, "that's what my friends are doing."

"Your friends are wasting their time too," she said. "You're all going to get married and this education is a foolish waste of money."

Since I was on a scholarship, this argument was on shaky ground. I said I was determined to stay on at school, and since it was free, my parents did not withdraw me.

The Wickedness of Working Independently

For years I had been writing. As a young child I invented a weekly family newspaper, which only lasted a few editions. I wrote it, laid it out in hand-drawn columns and drew the pictures.

Later, I wrote a monthly children's column for the synagogue newsletter. And in my teens I wrote articles for a Jewish magazine.

At school I wrote for the newspaper and the magazine, completed essays, stories and research papers. And I kept a journal, wrote poems, experimented with ideas.

It was clear where my interests lay. But I had no idea how to channel them.

As the end of my school years loomed ahead, I hoped desperately that I would pass my exams to take my place at London University. Even if I had to live at home at first, I was determined to be independent soon.

But I failed one of three exams, and was told to wait a year and reapply to college. My parents were quite relieved. I agreed to take a six-month secretarial course and work until I could start college.

After the course, I looked for a job. My interest in writing led to a job with a small publishing company. Eager to find the literary life, I started work as secretary to the sales manager.

I found little demand for literary talent in the office, where I wrote letters, filed invoices, retyped sales appeals, answered phone calls from irate salesmen, and saw manuscripts stacked ten-deep in the office, gathering dust.

For a day, I worked at the National Cat Show, handing out leaflets about "Cats in the Belfry," a best-selling company book. And once, I accompanied the garrulous disorganized sales manager to lunch at the best fish restaurant in town.

But there was no writing going on.

Through a friend, I met a reporter on a local weekly newspaper. She described to me what she did, and I thought it sounded like fun. She also told me how to get a job.

So I began writing letters, phoning and going to visit editors of weekly newspapers. By chance, a paper in Southend-on-Sea, part of a group of London papers, wanted a reporter. They hired me, and suddenly, I realized I was free.

I had to move the fifty miles from London to Southend. I had to find a room of my own in a boarding house. I had to work whatever hours the paper needed me. And I could choose my own style of life.

My parents were suitably shocked. But I was determined not to be dissuaded. I moved to Southend.

On my first day I went out to interview a couple celebrating their Golden Wedding after fifty years of marriage. I asked the twinkling-eyed husband how they had managed to stay together for so long. He said:

"I don't listen to her and she doesn't listen to me and we get along fine."

I went to Boy Scouts' fetes and church bazaars. I attended rock-and-roll concerts and summer theater. I interviewed ministers about church events, the police about crime, and the owners of the souvenir stands on the pier about the state of business. And I wrote them up on one of the ancient typewriters in the office on scraps of newsprint paper.

The staff of four had an editor, a tough but fair woman who had worked there for many years; an assistant editor in his thirties, who covered the courts and major events; a boy of about seventeen who loved horror movies and acted as copy boy; and a young man about my age who was also a new reporter, and interested in sports.

We worked in two dilapidated offices near the main street. And we were the second paper in town. The Big Weekly, as we thought of it, had a large circulation and an imposing building to match. Most people read the *Southend Standard,* not my epic prose in the *Southend Times.* My parents, who did not know how to explain this aberrant behavior, said I was working on *The Times* in Southend, to give the experience a touch of class.

Working on a newspaper is hardly paradise. But to me, there was a constant sense of exuberance. I was doing a job, and doing it well. I was learning a great deal. And I had broken away at last from the stranglehold of Orthodoxy. They couldn't drag me back and make me marry someone I didn't like. I did not have to stay home and cook and clean. I could earn my own money, pay my own rent, and lead my own life. I revelled in a sense of intoxication about the experience.

When I went home, there was fierce criticism. Both my parents felt the move was some kind of deranged experiment, a temporary roadblock. Then I would come home, meet a Nice Jewish Boy, get engaged, married and settle down.

I tried in vain to tell them what a good time I was having. My mother assumed I was living a life of constant debauchery.

"Can you take men back to your room?" she asked suspiciously.

I explained I was working, that I worked most evenings, and that I didn't know any men in Southend.

It was unheard of that I should be living on my own, and if I was, I must be doing naughty things. After all, isn't that what women are supposed to do?

Once you've been brainwashed to believe that women are sexual temptresses and totally incompetent, it's hard to imag-

ine that a woman might turn into a hard-working professional journalist. You assume that the one thing a woman
wants to do is sleep with men. The laws are clear on what
women mustn't do; therefore, once you've broken away, that
is what you must be doing.

It was oddly flattering to realize that by moving away from
home, I had become an irresistible woman of the world.
Though before I had never been the center of male attention, and was far from besieged by admirers, suddenly I had
a new image as a working woman, with men flocking to my
room and fighting to get into my bed.

The reality of my life was very different. My rented room
upstairs in a suburban house was plain and bare. My days
were long and exhausting, trekking around Southend and its
neighboring country communities by train and bus. And the
pressures of deadlines were constant.

But women locked inside Orthodoxy, unaware of the
world of work, and long brainwashed to see the outside as a
jungle of dangers, can only imagine the terrible things that
must be happening. They probably assumed that the reason
you didn't mention them was because they were too embarrassing to discuss.

As the weeks went by, I settled into the routine of work
and my own independent life. I came home occasionally, but
already I could sense a distance was being established between my family and my new life. I had my own work, my
own room, my own experiences.

The new division showed clearly when I agreed to attend a
cousin's Bar Mitzva party one Sunday afternoon. I came back
about halfway through. My mother was furious that I had
not come to the Sabbath ceremony. She was equally furious
that I planned to go back to Southend that evening.

"You have no respect for the family, or for the community," she said. "You should have been here all day. You
should have told them at work you have to come to a family
Bar Mitzva."

I didn't event want to argue with her. I understood why
she felt so obsessed with what had happened. In her mind,
there was no other role for me but to follow the rounds of

social events until I met and married. Then I could go on doing the same things with my husband. No matter how I behaved, no matter what I said, no matter how much I explained, she could not accept that I didn't want to be part of this narrow ghetto which trapped women like flies in amber.

Now that I'm older, I wonder too if there wasn't some jealousy mixed with my mother's anger. Here was her daughter, the one possession she could claim credit for besides her son, who was supposed to bring her happiness, fulfill her dreams, and whose wedding she had been planning since birth, going off in this strange and unacceptable direction.

What's more, I seemed to be enjoying it, thriving on the independence and showing capabilities that I wasn't supposed to possess.

Over the years that followed, I hung on to what I wanted to do. I lived and worked for a year in Israel. I worked in Paris for a news agency. I worked in Manchester for a daily newspaper, *The Guardian*. I coped with crises and cutbacks, firings and rehirings, finding apartments, packing and moving.

I had broken away from the Orthodoxy which had threatened to smother me. I had found my own independent path.

To prove to myself how free I was from the chains of Orthodoxy, I went out of my way to make sure I didn't observe a thing.

I asked to work on the Day of Atonement and the Jewish New Year, feeling that since I didn't want to keep them any longer, other people might take them off. I tried every possible kind of food that was offered to me. I went out with an amazing range of men from all kinds of backgrounds. And, in my first flush of rebellious freedom, I decided my religious upbringing didn't mean a thing to me.

But I learned you can't wipe out an intense experience like Orthodox Judaism. You can only slowly readjust to the saner view of life. You can rationally accept what you can live with and what you can't. And you learn to evaluate and sift the sensible from the crazy.

The biased teachings of those years had bred in me an automatic deferral to men. It's taken me years to learn not to accept the decision a man makes just because he is a man. I've had to force myself to respect my own judgment and not assume I must be wrong because I'm a woman. I've had to educate myself to see men as human beings, with feelings, emotions and attitudes which in some ways resemble mine and in other ways are different. And I've had to overcome the anger I felt against all men because of the one-sided view of the world Orthodox Judaism presented to me.

Patterns of Today

Orthodox and Hasidic women are still deprived of choices and options available to modern women, and see housekeeping, childrearing and homemaking as their roles. No one encourages them to go further. They continue to struggle on, with little education, with few opportunities for independence. Their daughters are still caught in the treadmill of Biblical behavior.

It's a sad reflection on the coming generation.

But to get out is a long and difficult struggle. You have to believe wholeheartedly that the constant message saying women are inferior, foolish and unclean is false. You have to believe that a woman has talent and abilities despite everything Orthodoxy teaches. And you have to believe that the unknown world outside the ghetto will give you greater happiness and satisfaction in life.

I don't know why I was so sure that it was true. I did know I couldn't accept the life I saw ahead of me which my mother and here friends so dutifully followed.

Among my own friends, many have accepted the Orthodox route. The boys I knew are the men running the synagogue. The girls are their wives, sitting upstairs in the ladies' gallery, smiling down in their mink coats as their mothers did before. The children learn the same outdated teachings. And little girls receive a second-hand Bat Mitzva, because they cannot be called to read from the scrolls.

Other friends took a different route. Some married, and then joined more liberal branches of Judaism. Rachel, now active in the Reform community, explained:

"I couldn't stand the snobbishness and exclusiveness of the Orthodox synagogue. They seemed to feel they were better than anyone else, and they always made me feel inferior. And I couldn't stand the way they didn't let the women get credit for all the work they did behind the scenes. Here, I sit with my family in the services, and our daughter has always been part of every celebration. It's so different, and much more what I can accept."

But some are caught in the middle. Miriam broke away from some of the more extreme practices of her ultra-religious family. She has a degree in sociology, a responsible position, and is married with two children.

She is constantly torn between the rational sense of knowing that much of the Orthodoxy in which she was raised is demeaning to women, and the pangs of her emotional ties to the observances and childhood patterns of behavior.

"How can you give it all up?" she asked me. "Don't you miss the celebrations? Don't you want to be part of the community? How can you put it all behind you?"

"I do what I want to do," I said. "I'm part of those communities where I feel comfortable. I can't accept sitting apart, being told what I can do as a woman, behaving like an inferior person."

"But don't you feel that the women who observe it all, who stay with the Orthodox community, are happier and more secure than we are?" she asked. "Everything is so settled for them."

"Baloney!" I replied firmly. "That's a myth and a smokescreen they like to erect. No woman who has to observe the laws which make her feel unclean, who has to do the hard physical work of cooking and cleaning nonstop, who has to obey the rules about keeping 'kosher' and who has no job or outside interest to give her a sense of her own worth is happy. She may say what she is told to say, but she has long ago given up her own identity and her own individuality and her own ability to understand what she wants. She's simply a robot repeating what she has been told. And she's bringing up a generation of children in total ignorance of the real world."

Miriam faced a conflict. The crisis came when her husband, equally observant, suddenly decided he wanted to change his life, go to college, and moved out. What's more, he moved in with a young girl a few years older than his teenage daughter. His family, their children and other friends rallied round Miriam, offering her help and encouragement during the pain. But her Orthodox relatives and her parents immediately blamed her.

"It's all your fault because you didn't go to the mikveh [ritual baths]," said her mother indignantly. "You didn't behave properly."

It's the fail-safe equation: "You must obey the Law of Orthodoxy to be happy. If you're unhappy, you didn't obey it enough."

Despite the years in which Miriam had been a devoted and observant Jewish wife, the years she had spent looking after their two children, the Passovers she had spent cleaning the house, and the hours she had spent in the synagogue services, she was immediately at fault for their husband's behavior.

To the Orthodox male perspective, the woman must always be in the wrong. It can't be the man's fault and it can't be the fault of the laws of Orthodoxy. It is the woman who did not do enough, did not give enough, did not submit enough.

Miriam struggled through a difficult time, feeling desperately guilty about the criticisms and angry at the attacks. She had little self-esteem because for years she had learned of her own inferior and unworthy status. It took a major breakdown and a period of intense counselling and psychotherapy before she regained her confidence. She slowly began to see that it was not her fault. The breakdown of the marriage was part of a chain of events. And in the end, it had been her husband who had selfishly disrupted all options for reconciliation, and left her to cope with the aftermath of the crisis.

I've asked her: "How can you go on observing the rules and believing in what you've learned after what you've been through?"

She shrugs. "I don't know how to give it up," she says, "it's been a part of me all my life."

Facing the Future

For the first time in human history, our generation of women is faced with unique choices. These choices are not confined to the elite few who can afford them. They are available to every woman in our society.

We are the recipient of new discoveries in health, new laws guaranteeing our security and fair treatment and of new attitudes toward women.

The very way we look and feel has changed dramatically. At a recent conference, several women in their fifties and sixties addressed the group.

"In literature and in the minds of men, women at this age are considered old crones," said one speaker. "But we are in the prime of our life. The reality is different from the fantasy. But the men have not understood the changes. For them, old is over thirty."

Ironically, men have not faced a revolution in their own lives. Instead they are adjusting to the changes in women's lives. They must rethink long-held prejudices and assumptions. They must change long-accepted patterns of behavior toward women.

For them, it's a revolution by reaction.

But for women, it is total revolution.

We are walking in uncharted territory. The traditional patterns of behavior have been challenged. What is the best path for us to choose?

There are no easy answers. Each woman must make her own decisions.

Women dare not see their rights to birth control and health information eroded. Women must not give up their education and professional training. Women cannot go back to the days of economic helplessness.

I see real danger in the ultra-Orthodox and Hasidic treatment of women. And I see this danger in the extremes of other anti-women religious groups.

I've found it hard to see much benefit for women in most religions. And I've read too much about the bloodshed, the battles and the cruelty committed in the name of religious passion or purity to believe it will ever bring peace to the world.

Women have moved forward steadily in this century. We cannot allow the religious zealots to turn back the clock. We may falter for a moment under the onslaught, but we must not take that as a signal for mass retreat.

History shows us what life was like in the past. We know what our grandmothers endured. We understand our achievements of today. And we have to speak out against repression, discrimination and bigotry that demean women, so that we can keep the freedom we have won for our daughters in the future.

If we do not, we may lose everything.

11

Epilogue

I knew I had to write this book after I went to my mother's funeral.

It was the first time in more than twenty years that I attended an Orthodox Jewish ceremony in the community where I grew up. After I broke away to work as a journalist, I didn't want to come back. Every now and then there would be family visits to my parents. I never attended services. I had forgotten what it was like.

But my mother died, and I went home for the funeral.

Suddenly I was back again, trapped in the past, being treated like a little girl, a helpless woman, a person with no rights and no standing in a male society.

On a damp, cold and bleak January day we attended the funeral service in the lofty, marble-floored hall at the Jewish cemetery. I held my father's arm to support him, a pale shaken man of eighty whose wife had always done everything for him. An official came over to steer me across the room, to where the women sat at one side. I must sit over there. I could not stay on this side with the men. A friend of my father sat with him on the bench.

The ceremony began after the minister arrived. He stood at the front facing the group of elderly men and women,

many of whom I'd known since childhood. The official ush-
ered my father and my brother to stand in front. I was allowed to stand to one side. My mother's only sister stood beside me. The official even beckoned my husband to stand in
front by the minister, though he's not Jewish. But as a man,
his status was clear.

The service was solemn but brief. The minister extolled
my mother as an exemplary wife and mother, a devoted
member of the synagogue Ladies' Guild, a tireless community worker and volunteer. The coffin, covered by a black
cloth, stood in front of us. The prayers ended. The doors behind opened. With the help of the family, the coffin on its
trolley was pushed out into the frigid air, along paths, across
a road and past the expanse of marble gravestones which
covered the once rolling green acres of fields.

Behind came the men of the community. And far behind,
the women, dutifully hanging back. At the graveside, there
were more prayers. Then the coffin was lowered into its hole.
The minister took the spade and shovelled a handful of
earth on top. My brother and father followed him. Other
men in the community did the same. I moved forward
calmly, took the spade and threw some earth on to the coffin.
No other woman moved from her place.

We drove back to the house. For a week, we observed the
traditional mourning, sitting on special chairs, not going out,
waiting for friends to visit, attending the morning and evening prayer services.

The first evening as the prayers began, my brother tried to
herd the women out into the hall. I was horrified. Here was a
mourning ceremony for a woman. Here were many of her
friends, also women. Here was her sister, a woman in her
seventies. And here was I, her only daughter, sent outside as
if we were unworthy of participation in prayers. "I refuse to
stay in the hall," I said firmly. "The women can stand in the
back of the room."

There were a few mumbles. But I knew that it was quite
permissible for women to be in the room. They were not allowed to pray or sing aloud. Nor could they lead the services.
But they could be present.

The women said nothing, but filed in and squeezed into the back of the room. The men chanted and muttered their way through the evening prayers, and the special mourners' invocations.

The rest of the week was like watching a replay of the years of my past. Friends I remembered as teenagers came to call with their teenage children. Their parents who remembered me as a child, came to reminisce. The warm enveloping friendliness had not changed. Nor had the undertones of craziness.

One woman prayed in the hall, not believing that she had the right to stand in the back of the room. Another arrived wearing a wig, long sleeves and a high-collared blouse, placing her chair conspicuously away from the others, lest she touch anyone else.

They asked about my husband and my children. I replied. I was a wife and a mother. That was acceptable. I, as a person, an individual, a journalist, did not exist.

Nor did I exist as a person when they counted for the *minyan*, the ten men necessary before prayers can be recited. As the week passed, the weather became colder. One morning there were only nine men for the prayers. Of course, I was there, since I came over early every morning from my cousin's where I was staying. My bother, agitated and angry that there was no *minyan*, told me to call several of my father's friends to round up the requisite number.

As I made the telephone calls to these old men, I felt as if I was an actor in a bizarre movie. There were ten people in the house. But one of them happened to be a woman. And I did not exist, I had to persuade an elderly man to come out on this bitter cold morning, because he was a Real Person and counted as one, to make up the ten required. Once again, I had become a Non-person.

The Sabbath provided new reminders of the past. I reverted to my role of "Shabbas Goy"—a person who, like a non-Jew carries out the duties that the ultra-Orthodox won't perform on the Sabbath.

I prepared a warm meal for my father when he came back from the synagogue. I heated water for tea. I turned the heating on and off. I turned the lights on and off. I answered the phone.

These are tasks the ultra-Orthodox believe should not be done on the Sabbath. I always thought the rules were foolish. My father and my brother made no comment.

At the evening service on the Sabbath, a man known for his Biblical interpretations spoke. He sat at the front of the room, and said his theme was the goodness of women. He was a round man, with glasses, and a loud voice. The room was quite crowded with friends of my parents.

He began with a Talmudic legend of a man lying in bed who sees a woman flying out of a window, and who then finds himself flying out of a window. The story rambled on, embellished with obscure details. The men, sitting at the front, nodded and chuckled. The women at the back, where I sat, were stoically silent.

It was like listening to an entertaining maniac in a lunatic asylum. You have no idea what he's talking about, but you might as well listen. I felt as if I was sitting in the middle of a Chagall painting of a Russian village in the last century, quite detached from reality.

By the end of the week I was suffocating. I began counting the hours until I could go home to my life, and my wonderfully sane husband and children and friends. I considered the idea of leaving earlier than I had planned.

But I stayed. I helped my father the way a Good Jewish Daughter is supposed to. I shopped, cleared out my mother's clothes, organized the food deliveries from the butcher and the grocer. I accepted some jewelry which my father wanted me to have. I listened to the endless discussions about the proper inscription for the prayerbooks which my father would donate to the synagogue in his wife's memory. I offered as much sensible advice as my father could manage. And I tried to ease myself back into the mindset of subservience and dutifulness.

It was like being trapped in a strange dream world of existence. I was a grown person, capable of responsibility and achievement in my own right. I had traveled, married, raised two children, worked in many demanding positions. And here I was back again, feeling the same sensation of walking through thick syrup, caught and unable to move, that I remembered from my years of adolescence.

It was as if I could slip back into the past without missing a beat. I only had to observe a few rules, give up foolish ideas about women's independence, and everything would be just as it used to be, in the good old days.

The hours crawled by. My brother left to go home. I stayed to help with clearing out some old photographs, seeing the lawyer with my father, talking to him about coping on his own, giving my phone number to friends of his in the apartment building. Finally, it was time to leave.

I flew back home in a mood of intense excitement. I felt a sense of liberation, as if I had just escaped from prison. I arrived at our house in the middle of the day. No one was there.

I walked from room to room, exulting aloud:

"I'm home! I'm home! I'm home!"

It had taken me a long time to get there.

Glossary

Adonai   The Lord God.

Agunah   A woman who cannot remarry because her husband has not given her a religious divorce bill.

Bar Mitzva   Ceremony of entry into adult male world for boys of thirteen; meaning "Son of the Commandment."

Bat Mitzva   Ceremony for twelve- or thirteen-year-old girls; meaning "Daughter of the Commandment."

Bimah   Platform, stage. Raised area in synagogue.

Bris/Brit Milah   Covenant of Circumcision performed on male babies a week after birth.

Daven, Daveners.   To pray. People praying, reciting prayers.

Devekut   Clinging to God. The Hasidic description of the emotional style of prayer they advocate.

Elohim, Elokim.   Hebrew word for "God," and its changed form used to avoid taking God's name in vain.

Fleishig   Yiddish for "meat," usually referring to the distinction between meat and milk dishes.

Get   Religious bill of divorce.

Goy   Non-Jew, singular form.

Goyim   Non-Jews, plural.

Haggadah   Book used at Passover service to tell the story of the Jews' escape from slavery in Egypt.

Halachah   Laws; the complete body of Jewish law.

Hallah   Special part of dough made by women; also, loaves used on Sabbath.

Minyan   Quorum of ten men necessary for prayer.

Hashem   The Name; used to avoid saying God's name in vain when studying Hebrew texts.

Hasid   A learned man.

Hasidim   Sect of Jews which began about 1730s, created by Baal Shem Tov, in Poland.

Ketuba   Religious marriage contract.

Ketuvim   Writings; refers to part of Bible which includes Psalms and Proverbs.

Kibbutz   Collective farm in Israel.

Kosher   Refers to food which meets Jewish dietary laws.

Kitsur Shulhan Aruch   Code of Jewish Law, compiled in 16th century by Joseph Caro.

Matzoh   Unleavened bread, eaten during festival of Passover.

Mazeltov!   Good luck! Congratulations!

Mikveh   Ritual bath.

Milchig   Yiddish for "milk," usually referring to distinction between meat and milk dishes.

Mishnah   Part of written commentary in the Talmud.

Mitzva, Mitzvot   A good deed or deeds; also a commandment or observance.

Mohel   Man who performs religious circumcision

Neveeim   Prophets; refers to the section of the Bible after the first five books; deals with prophets.

Niddah   Separation. The laws which require separation of women during their menstrual cycle.

Pareve   Either-Or. Food and utensils which can be used either for milk or for meat.

Pidyon Haben   Redemption of the Firstborn. The ceremony for baby boys when they are more than 30 days old.

Seder   Order. Describes service on evening of Passover when Haggadah is read.

Shtetl   Yiddish word for small community in Eastern Europe.

Siddur   Order; the Jewish prayer book.

Simhat Torah   Rejoicing of the Law. The celebration of the annual conclusion of weekly readings from the Torah.

Shabbat   Jewish Sabbath, which begins at nightfall on Friday and ends at nightfall on Saturday.

Shiksa   Non-Jewish woman, usually used in derogatory sense.

Shofar   Ram's horn, sounded on Jewish New Year and Day of Atonement.

Sotah   Punishment for women suspected of adultery in Temple times (Numbers 5:11-31).

Taharat Ha Mishpahah   Purity of the Family. The Niddah laws together with other laws for women concerning modesty.

Talmud   The interpretation and commentary on the Torah.

Tefillah   Prayer.

T'nack   The Hebrew equivalent of the Old Testament Bible; includes the Torah, the prophets and writings.

Torah   The first five books of the Bible (Genesis, Exodus, Leviticus, Numbers, Deuteronomy), often called the five books of Moses.

Trefa   Any food which is not permitted under Jewish dietary laws.

Yeshivah   Jewish academy for religious studies.

Zaddik   Wise man, learned in Hebrew studies.

Zuzim   Ancient silver coins.

Short Bibliography

Resource Texts

The Bible (Old Testament) Revised Standard Version.

Code of Jewish Law: A Compilation of Jewish Laws and Customs, by Rabbi Solomon Ganzfried (Hebrew Publishing Company, New York: 1963).

Taharas Am Yisroel. A Guide to the Laws of "Taharas Hamishpochoh" (Family Purity), by Rabbi S. Wagschal (Philipp Feldheim Inc., New York: 1982).

Halichos Bas Yisrael. A Woman's Guide to Jewish Observance, Vol. 1, by Rav Yitzchak Yaacov Fuchs. English edition prepared by Rav Moshe Dombey, in collaboration with the author (Targum Press Inc., Michigan: 1985).

From the Teaching of Our Sages: A Compendium of Insights, Homilies, and Interpretations of the Weekly Sedra, by Rabbi Mordechai Katz (JEP Publications, New York: 1978).

General Books

American Judaism (Second Edition), by Nathan Glazer (University of Chicago Press: 1972).

The Second Jewish Catalog, compiled and edited by Sharon Strassfeld and Michael Strasfeld (Jewish Publication Society of America, Philadelphia: 1976).

Heritage; Civilization and the Jews, by Abba Eban (Summit Books, New York: 1984).

Hasidism: Popular History of Jewish Civilization, compiled by Aryeh Rubinstein (Leon Amiel Publisher, New York/Paris: 1975).

Women and Family

The Jewish Home, compiled by members of the Publications Committee of the Jewish Marriage Education Council.

Marital Relations, Birth Control and Abortion in Jewish Law, by David M. Feldman (Schocken Books, New York: 1974).

On Being A Jewish Feminist: A Reader, edited by Susannah Heschel (Schocken Books, New York: 1983).

The Jewish Woman: New Perspectives, edited by Elizabeth Koltun (Schocken Books, New York: 1976).

Jewish Woman in Jewish Law, by Moshe Meiselman (Ktav Publishing House, New York: 1978).

Judaism and the New Woman, by Rabbi Sally Preisand (Behrman House, Inc., New York: 1975).

Jewish and Female: Choices and Changes in Our Lives Today, by Susan Weidman Schneider (Simon & Schuster, New York: 1984).

Pardes Rimonim: A Marriage Manual for the Jewish Family, by Moshe David Tendler (The Judaica Press, Inc., New York: 1982).

Major Jewish Groups

Union of American Hebrew Congregations (Reform)
838 Fifth Avenue, New York, N.Y. 10021

United Synagogue of America (Conservative)
155 Fifth Avenue, New York, N.Y. 10010

Jewish Reconstructionist Foundation (Reconstructionist)
31 East 28 Street, New York, N.Y. 10016

Union of Orthodox Jewish Congregations of America (Orthodox)
45 West 36 Street, New York, N.Y. 10018.